Water for the Soul

NATIONAL DISTRIBUTORS

AUSTRALIA: CMC Australasia, PO Box 519, Belmont, Victoria 3216. Tel: (03) 5241 3288

CANADA: CMC Distribution Ltd., PO Box 7000, Niagara on the Lake, Ontario L0S 1J0. Tel: 1 800 325 1297

INDIA: Full Gospel Literature Stores, 254 Kilpauk Garden Road, Chennai 600010. Tel: (44) 644 3073

KENYA: Keswick Bookshop, PO Box 10242, Nairobi. Tel: (02) 331692/226047

MALAYSIA: Salvation Book Center (M), 23 Jalan SS2/64, Sea Park, 47300 Petaling Jaya, Selangor. Tel: (3) 7766411

NEW ZEALAND: CMC New Zealand Ltd., PO Box 949, 205 King Street South, Hastings. Tel: (6) 8784408; Toll free: 0800 333639

NIGERIA: FBFM, (Every Day with Jesus), Prince's Court, 37 Ahmed Onibudo Street, PO Box 70952, Victoria Island. Tel: 01 2617721, 616832

REPUBLIC OF IRELAND: Scripture Union, 40 Talbot Street, Dublin 1. Tel: (01) 8363764

SINGAPORE: Campus Crusade Asia Ltd., 315 Outram Road, 06–08 Tan Boon Liat Building, Singapore 169074. Tel: (65) 222 3640

SOUTH AFRICA: Struik Christian Books (Pty Ltd), PO Box 193, Maitland 7405, Cape Town. Tel: (021) 551 5900

SRI LANKA: Christombu Investments, 27 Hospital Street, Colombo 1. Tel: (1) 433142/328909

USA: Broadman & Holman Publishers, 127 Ninth Avenue, North, Nashville, Tennessee 37234 Tel: (800) 251 3225

EVERY DAY Light™

Daily Inspirations

From

SELWYN HUGHES

VIGNETTES PAINTED BY

THOMAS KINKADE

———————— ⟡ ————————

NASHVILLE, TENNESSEE

EVERY DAY LIGHT text 1998 © Selwyn Hughes
EVERY DAY LIGHT illustrations © 1998 Thomas Kinkade, Media Arts Group Inc., San Jose, CA
Section Introductions: Leonard G. Goss

Published by Broadman & Holman Publishers, Nashville, TN
Acquisitions and Development Editor: Leonard G. Goss
Design: CWR Production
Typesetting: David Poyser, Reading, England

0-8054-1774-5
Dewey Decimal Classification: 242.2
Subject Heading: DEVOTIONAL EXERCISES

Unless otherwise indicated, all Scripture references are from the Holy Bible: New International
Version: Copyright © 1973, 1978, 1984 the International Bible Society. Used by permission of
Zondervan Bible Publishers.

Every Day Light
Material taken from editions of Every Day with Jesus previously published as follows:
Staying Spiritually Fresh 1987,   Rebuilding Broken Walls 1995,
The Character of God 1994,   When Sovereignty Surprises 1992,
The Fruit of the Spirit 1987,   Seven Pillars of Wisdom 1993

Further Study section compiled by Trevor J. Partridge; day 60–121 by David Gurney.

Previously published by CWR as *Every Day with Jesus* – One Year Devotional copyright © 1998

CWR, Waverley Abbey House, Waverley Lane, Farnham, Surrey, England

Contents   Page

Foreword

As a painter, I spend a lot of time studying the effect of light. It's the source of a painting's visual expression; it is also a sign of warmth, hospitality, and sanctuary. Though there are usually several light sources in a scene, one source must predominate – sunset over the ocean perhaps, or the gaslights of a city street, or a cheerful fire in a country cottage. With illumination from a single direction, highlights and shadows all fall into their proper places, and the whole scene takes on a sense of order and completeness.

The spiritual world also has a single source of light – the light of God's truth as revealed in Scripture. Without it we would find ourselves stumbling along in an abstract existence of shadows and confusion, with no sense of direction nor understanding of God's perfect plan.

In this new edition of *Every Day Light*, it is my pleasure once again to follow Selwyn Hughes on a spiritually illuminating journey through daily Bible reading, prayer, and inspiring commentary in search of God's light for our lives. Over two generations, his writings and sermons have led millions of hearts in Britain and other parts of the world to a clearer application of the Gospel. Our first publication of *Every Day Light* was greeted in America with an enthusiasm that has touched us both deeply, and has now led him to offer this fresh and completely new study for his newfound friends on this side of the Atlantic.

Following the style of its predecessor, this devotional guide presents a full year's worth of readings, arranged so you can start them any day of the year. Each entry paints a picture in words of the world God has in store for us, leading us toward the one true light that guides our path unerringly to Him.

Thomas Kinkade

Introduction

ittle did I realize in 1965 when I set out to write a series of scripturally-based thoughts, at the request of a few Christians in the church I then pastored, that this would grow and develop into what it has become today – a daily devotional read in 120 countries and available in some twenty languages.

This second (special) one-year edition brings together some of the themes that over the years have proved most popular with *Every Day wih Jesus* readers. I have always been able to tell which themes touch people's lives most powerfully by the number of letters I receive from my readers. The six themes presented in this volume are amongst some of the most well received of all that I have written.

Many Christians complain that sometimes they go through periods of spiritual dryness and staleness. *Staying Spiritually Fresh* – the first theme on the list – will help you move toward maintaining the spiritual glow despite the circumstances in which you find yourself. *Rebuilding Broken Walls* will take you into the thrilling story of Nehemiah. I received some incredible testimonies following the first presentation of this theme.

The Character of God will give you a glimpse into the nature of our great God and will, I believe, set you on fire to become more and more like Him. The book of Ruth is a favorite with most Christians and I think you will find *When Sovereignty Surprises* a satisfying feast. *The Fruit of the Spirit* and *The Seven Pillars of Wisdom* have blessed hundreds of thousands of God's people. The latter draws out principles from the book of Proverbs and has been reprinted several times.

My prayer and wish is that all these themes will delight and bless you too – and lead you into a fuller, deeper and richer daily relationship with our Lord.

Selwyn Hughes

Topical Index

Topical Index (continued)

SECTION ONE

Staying
Spiritually Fresh

Staying Spiritually Fresh

⁕

The subjects Thomas Kinkade most enjoys painting – cottages, street scenes, country churches, gardens – have already been painted many times. His challenge is to keep them fresh by introducing touches that portray the familiar in a new way. In this first section of *Every Day Light*, Selwyn Hughes addresses our need to stay fresh as Christians in a stale world by leading us to Bible verses that underscore the restorative powers of the spirit.

Sometimes Selwyn suggests a new way of looking at well-known verses, such as the powerful and inspiring words of Paul in Romans, Colossians, and Philippians. In other lessons he highlights references many readers may be unfamiliar with, including the Old Testament books of Malachi and 1 Kings. In every case his examples clarify the biblical point with a precision that makes reading them both exciting and unforgettable.

There is no better image for renewal than the one Selwyn presents on the very first page – a watered garden in the desert as described in Isaiah 58. We are called to be gardens of faith in the dry desert of an apathetic – even hostile – environment. Christians often find themselves moving in opposition to what the rest of society is doing. But what a joy it is to refresh a thirsty world with the life-giving waters of Scripture once we understand that is God's direction.

Life is a kaleidoscope of changing relationships and opportunities that give us new ways to express, celebrate, and affirm our faith every day. To that end, Selwyn identifies twelve principles which will keep our outlook fresh and vital even in what appears to be a barren spiritual plain. With God's help, we can boldly remove the barriers that keep us from experiencing, enjoying, and sharing the message of the love of Christ. Our success at putting faith into practice doesn't depend on how eager non-Christians are to accept us, but on the strength and purity of our own spiritual wellspring.

L.G.G.

Fresh water!

"When it empties into the Sea, the water there becomes fresh." (v.8)

For reading & meditation – Ezekiel 47:1–12

*O*ur subject is a challenging but deeply inspiring one – *Staying Spiritually Fresh*. The idea for this theme arose out of a letter I received some time ago which said: "Over the past year or so, my Christian life has become stale – insufferably so. I have lost the freshness and spontaneity I once knew. Can you say something that will help bring back the sparkle into my Christian experience? What is the remedy?"

I want to introduce you to twelve principles which, when put into practice, will enable you to maintain spiritual freshness even though around you all may be stale and arid. They have worked for me for over forty years – I believe they will also work for you. But can we expect always to live in a state of spiritual alertness and freshness? Isn't that being unrealistically optimistic? Well, what does Scripture say? It shows that the people of God are meant to be beautiful gardens in the midst of a dry desert. The prophet Isaiah puts it like this: "And you shall be like a watered garden and like a spring of water whose waters fail not" (Isa. 58:11, Amplified Bible).

In our text for today, Ezekiel speaks of the river flowing "into the Dead Sea, into the brackish waters which shall turn fresh" (Moffatt). How thrilling. The river of God flowing into our dead seas turns them fresh. Whatever reasons there are for our lives becoming spiritually stale, it is quite clear from Scripture that they need not be so. God offers to exchange His strength daily for our weakness, His freshness for our staleness. Let's go for it.

FURTHER STUDY

John 4:1–29; 7:37–38;
Rev. 7:17

1. What is the quality of the water that Christ gives?

2. How did Jesus describe it to the woman?

 Prayer

My Father and my God, I come at the beginning of these meditations to ask that You will make my life like a watered garden. Let Your fresh rivers run into my dead seas so that my whole being is revived – day after day after day. Amen.

The morning watch

"Very early in the morning ... Jesus ... went off to a solitary place, where he prayed." (v.35)

For reading & meditation – Mark 1:32–45

e began yesterday with the exciting thought that whatever reasons exist for spiritual staleness – it need not be so. Spiritual freshness is available to us all – and on a daily basis. However, maintaining spiritual freshness does not mean that we will be exempted from having to face occasional trials and difficulties. It means, rather, that no matter how dry and difficult our circumstances, our experience of God can remain fresh and vibrant.

What, then, is the first principle of maintaining spiritual freshness? This – establish a daily quiet time with God in order to replenish your spiritual resources. Some modern-day Christians balk at this idea. They say, "The Lord is with us all the time, so why do we need to fence off a particular part of the day to spend time with Him? A daily quiet time can soon bring one into legalism." I am well aware of that danger, but again I say – it need not be so. There have been periods in my own life when my quiet time was nothing more than a ritual, but that was more a consequence than a cause.

FURTHER STUDY

Psa. 119:137–148;
5:1–3;
Gen. 28:18;
Dan. 6:10

1. When did the psalmist pray?

2. When do you pray?

The best period for a quiet time, in my opinion, is in the morning – before the day starts. Some prefer the evening, or perhaps, as in the case of busy mothers and wives, the late morning, when the family has left and the house is quiet. Each must establish the best time according to preference or convenience. A certain time of the day ought not to belong to the day. It belongs to the getting of resources for the day. Start the day right and you will end it right.

✦ *Prayer* ✦

O God, help me to see that just as I need to take time out of the day to feed myself physically, so I need to take time out to feed myself spiritually. Help me not just to acknowledge this, but to act on it. In Christ's Name I pray. Amen.

The standard note

*"Let the morning bring me word of your unfailing love, for I
have put my trust in you." (v.8)*

For reading & meditation – Psalm 143:1–12

*W*e continue meditating on the need for a daily quiet
time in order to replenish our spiritual resources.
Jesus felt the need for three simple habits: (1) He
stood up to read; (2) He went up a mountain to pray; (3) He taught
people the Scriptures; all "as His custom was." These three habits
– reading and meditating in the Scriptures, exposing oneself to
God in prayer, and passing on to others what one has found – are
as basic in the spiritual life as two and two make four is in
mathematics. If Jesus couldn't get along without them – how can
we?

I am often asked by interviewers how I maintain my spiritual
life. I usually reply that it centers on a daily quiet time with God.
There are some days when a morning quiet time is not possible,
but most of my mornings begin with a time closeted with God in
prayer. Someone sent me a brochure telling me of a home that had
opened which they described as "a place in the country where
those who have lost their spiritual freshness may come to tone up
and be invigorated." My quiet time is such a "place."

A sheep rancher in Australia found that his violin was out of
tune, and being unable to find another musical instrument to
provide him with a standard note, he wrote to a radio station
asking them to strike that note. They did just that – stopped a
program and struck the note. The sheep rancher caught it and the
violin was in tune again. Your daily quiet time will help you hear
God's "standard notes." Then you can tune your flattened notes to
His.

FURTHER STUDY

Acts 10:1–8;
Luke 6:12;
2 Chron. 29:2

1. What is recorded of
Cornelius?

2. What is said about
Hezekiah?

⇥ *Prayer* ⇤

*O God, I know there is nothing better than I have found in You – except more
of what I have found in You. Help me today to catch Your "standard note" and
tune every part of my life to it. In Christ's Name I ask it. Amen.*

"Children of the dawn"

"O thou Eternal, show us favor ... be our strong arm, morn after morn ..." (v.2, Moffatt)

For reading & meditation – Isaiah 33:1–24

Those who do not provide for a time during the day, preferably in the morning, when they can replenish their spiritual resources, may find that they have to provide a time at the end of the day for regret, for repentance, and for eating humble pie.

A traveler in the Himalayas tells how he arose very early one morning to watch the sun rise on the towering peaks. He says: "There, as the day began to dawn, we saw arise before our enraptured gaze, within a complete semicircle, twenty peaks each above twenty thousand feet in height, snow-capped with virgin snow. For half an hour the curtain was lifted and we inwardly worshiped. Then the mists began to fill the valleys between and the view was gone. Gone? No, not really – it was forever laid up in our green and grateful memories."

That is what a quiet time in the early part of the day does for you. Before the mists of worldly happenings blot out your view of God, you take a time exposure of Him which is indelibly imprinted on your mind. Then, after the mists close in, the vision is there – within. You live in two worlds at once – drawing physical strength from the world around you, and spiritual sustenance from the world above you. Pascal, the great French philosopher and Christian, once said: "Nearly all the ills of life spring from this simple source: that we are not able to sit still in a room." But what if, in the stillness, we meet with God – how healing that would be. We would arise with what Stevenson calls "happy morning faces." We become children of the dawn.

FURTHER STUDY

Lam. 3:22–26;
Psa. 40:1;
Isa. 26:8

1. What was the psalmist's testimony?

2. What did the psalmist say he would do?

⊷⊷ *Prayer* ⊷⊷

Heavenly Father, give me the wisdom to be able to take "the pause that refreshes," to drink every day from the living Fountain, the Eternal spring. In Jesus' Name I pray. Amen.

How to organize a quiet time

"For God alone my soul waits in silence, for my hope is from him." (v.5, RSV)

For reading & meditation – Psalm 62:1–12

Someone has described the morning quiet time as "turning the dial until we tune in to God's wavelength – then we get the message." But how do we gain the best results from our quiet time?

First, decide on the amount of time you want to give to waiting before God. Next, take your Bible and read a portion slowly. Let it soak in. If some words or verses strike you, focus on them in meditation. They will yield up new meanings to you. Write these down. After the reading, let go, relax and say to Him: "Father, have You anything to say to me?" *Learn to listen.* All those who hear God's voice on a regular basis say that it is something they have had to develop. They pause, they wait, and they learn after a while to disentangle their own thoughts from what God is saying. Then speak to God in prayer. Finally, thank Him for the answer. He always answers – whether it is "Yes," "No" or "Wait." "No" is just as much an answer as "Yes" – sometimes a better answer.

Not far from my home is the River Thames. Sometimes I walk along the river bank and watch small boats entering the locks. These boats come along the adjoining rivers and, to get into the Thames, they have to enter the lock and wait there to be lifted up to a higher level. The quiet time does that – it shuts you in with God. But then infinite resources begin to bubble up from below and you are lifted silently and without strain on to a higher level. The lifting is the result of being shut in with God.

FURTHER STUDY

Psa. 130:1–8;
27:14; 37:7;
Isa. 30:18

1. What do we often find the hardest thing to do?

2. Take time out today to do this.

⊹⊱ *Prayer* ⊰⊹ ---

O Father, help me resolve to try every day to spend a quiet time with You. May my quiet time at this moment be the open door through which I glide out on to a higher level of life. In Jesus' Name I ask it. Amen.

Sand in the machinery of living

"But now you must rid yourselves of ... anger, rage, malice, slander and filthy language ..." (v.8)

For reading & meditation – Colossians 3:1–15

*A*nother thing we must do if we are to maintain spiritual freshness is to determine to forgive everyone who hurts us and refuse to nurse a grudge. Grudges become glooms.

A few years after World War II, a Christian Japanese boy at a public speaking contest announced his subject as "The Sacredness of Work." Some people smiled at his choice, but when they heard his story their smiles turned to tears. His parents and home were burned to ashes in the atomic bomb explosion at Nagasaki. He was the eldest of three surviving children, and together they knelt in the ashes of their home and prayed to know what to do. One of them said: "I know – we can work." So they set to work, gathering bits of tin and boards, and soon they had a little hut in which to live. They could have nursed their grudge and become gloomy; instead they forgave, forgot and went to work.

No one who wants to maintain spiritual freshness can afford to nurse a grudge. It will poison both spirit and body. As one doctor put it: "Grudges ... put the whole physical and mental system on a war basis, instead of on a peace basis." Walter Alvarez, a medical doctor and a counselor, says: "I often tell patients they cannot afford to carry grudges or maintain hates. Such things can make them ill and tire them out. I once saw a man kill himself inch by inch, simply by thinking of nothing but hatred for a relative who had sued him. Within a year or two he was dead." A grudge or a resentment is sand in the machinery of living.

FURTHER STUDY

Eph. 4:21–32;
Rom. 3:14;
Heb. 12:15

1. What should not come out of our mouths?

2. What are we to do?

⊷ *Prayer* ⊷

O Father, teach me how to get the splinters of resentment out of my soul and also out of my body. Help me to decide that it is the oil of love, not the sand of resentments, that shall go into the machinery of my life day by day. Amen.

"He burns me up"

"Let us keep the Festival, not with ... malice and wickedness, but with sincerity and truth." (v.8)

For reading & meditation – 1 Corinthians 5:1–13

*I*s it true that nursing a grudge can cause physical illness? A man I knew became enraged over something another Christian had done to him. I advised him to forgive and forget. He replied: "But every time I see him, he burns me up." I said: "That's because you want to burn him up and all you succeed in doing is burning yourself up." I told him about the sadistic farmer who tied a small stick of dynamite to a hawk, lit the fuse and then turned it loose, expecting it to blow itself up in mid-air. Instead, the hawk flew into his barn and the explosion wrecked, not only the barn, but part of his house also.

He listened, but I could see my words had not gone in. He could think and talk of nothing else but getting even with his fellow Christian. His wife told me that his breath became foul, his appetite left him, his digestion became bad, he suffered loss of sleep and, after a few months, he dropped down dead.

In case someone says, "But there could have been other reasons for his death," I can tell you that I talked to his doctor, a close personal friend of mine, and he told me that the man had died of an "undrained grudge." Of course, you can't put that on a death certificate, but many doctors know that "undrained grudges" play a major role in creating physical disorders. A missionary suffered a breakdown because of a grudge he had held against his organization for not supplying him with enough money. Apparently grudges are just as deadly in the godly as the ungodly.

FURTHER STUDY

1 John 2:1–11;
Prov. 10:12;
Isa. 59:9–10

1. What brings us back into darkness?
2. What is the result of walking in darkness?

⤐ *Prayer* ⤐

Father, I see so clearly that my hurts hurt me even more when I harbor them. Help me not to hold on stubbornly to my wounded pride, but consent for You to lance my inner boils, no matter how much it may hurt. In Jesus' Name. Amen.

"We become what we give out"

"Do not answer a fool according to his folly, or you will be like him yourself." (v.4)

For reading & meditation – Proverbs 26:1–12

We continue to look at the effect of grudges and resentment on the personality. Karl Menninger says: "I know from clinical experience that in some women, the degree of discomfort both in pregnancy and parturition (childbirth) has been directly proportional to the intensity of their resentment at having to live through this phase of the female role."

Sometimes resentments and grudges can be unconscious. As one doctor put it: "It is very difficult to get people to see that illness is the price they pay for their unconscious resentments toward the very things they protest they love." A woman of sixty-five gave her heart to Christ and said: "I've lived with a stone in my heart ever since my mother said she hated me for stopping her going to another man. Now that stone has gone. I'm free – for the first time in almost half a century."

A man gave a golf ball the name of someone he disliked and struck it – but the ball went into the rough. If you bear a grudge against anyone, you can't see straight, or drive straight. The fact is this – you just cannot hurt another person without hurting yourself. As the Chinese put it: "He who spits against the wind spits in his own face." We become the product of the qualities we give out. If we give out evil in return for good, then we become evil; we become the thing we give out. If we give out good for evil, then we become the product of what we give out – we become good. So mark this and mark it well – you cannot maintain spiritual freshness while you are bearing a grudge.

FURTHER STUDY

Rom. 12:1–17;
Lev. 19:18;
Prov. 20:22

1. What are we not to do?

2. What are we not to say?

⇥ *Prayer* ⇤

Heavenly Father, I see that I cannot be an echo of the treatment people give to me. I must echo You and treat people as You treat them. But I cannot do this except by Your grace. I receive that grace now. Amen.

Stop corroding your soul

"... Do not let the sun go down while you are still angry ..."
(v.26)

For reading & meditation – Ephesians 4:22–32

We continue meditating on the truth that grudges are sand in the machinery of life. We cannot maintain our spiritual freshness if resentment is allowed to fester in our hearts.

The Christian faith makes it quite clear that whatever shuts out our brother or sister also shuts out our Father. Look at the orders given to us by our Lord: "So if when you are offering your gift at the altar you there remember that your brother has any grievance against you, leave your gift at the altar and go. First make peace with your brother, and then come back and present your gift" (Matt. 5:23–24, Amplified Bible). Stop all religious observance, says Jesus; it is useless if you are not attempting to be reconciled to your brother. For shutting out our brother shuts out our Father – automatically.

What about when we have a grievance against our brother? This: "If your brother sins against you, go and show him his fault, just between the two of you" (Matt. 18:15). Whether we have sinned against our brother or our brother has sinned against us, we are under an obligation to settle it – *as far as we are concerned*. Our brother may not respond but that is not our responsibility. A Christian must not just go halfway to settle a quarrel – he must go all the way. Whatever shuts out your brother shuts out your Father. Grudges have no place in a Christian heart. Let the text at the top of this page take hold of you today, and don't keep a grudge overnight – for if you do, you will wake up in the morning with a corroded soul.

FURTHER STUDY

Matt. 5:38–48;
Prov. 24:29;
1 Pet. 3:9

1. How are we to repay evil?

2. How are we to treat our enemies?

❧ *Prayer* ❧

O God, help me, for I know that grudges and resentments can so blind me that I cannot see straight. Give me grace to relinquish all grudges that are within me – now. For Jesus' sake. Amen.

Leave vengeance to God

"The Spirit of the Lord is on me ... to proclaim the year of the Lord's favor." (vv.18–19)

For reading & meditation – Luke 4:14–30

Now and again I stress heavily this matter of grudges, because I have found that this is a truth which always brings a positive response

Following some remarks I made concerning an unforgiving spirit, a woman wrote: "I had often read in *Every Day with Jesus* your words about forgiveness, and I knew that one day I would have to face up to this challenge. Today's reading demolished all my defenses. Intellectually I had always accepted what you said about the need to forgive and that I could not be whole until I had completely forgiven those who had hurt me, but I wouldn't get down to actually putting it into words. I kept holding back my feelings, saying subconsciously: 'I will some day and then my troubles will be over – but not yet.' Your words today came like a bolt from the blue: 'There is usually a reason why we don't want to give up our grudges and resentments – one reason is that we use them to feel sorry for ourselves.' I certainly had done my share of that, but suddenly – I let go. It was like a boil bursting. All the pent-up poisons gushed out of me and I was a new person. I'm in the midst of a campaign now to overcome the misunderstandings of years."

What happened to that woman can happen now, today, to you. No matter how wronged you have been – forgive. When Jesus announced His mission in Nazareth, He read from Isaiah's prophecy until He came to the words, "the day of vengeance of our God." Then He closed the book. You do the same. Leave vengeance to God – use only redemptive goodwill.

FURTHER STUDY

Mark 11:18–25;
Luke 11:4; 17:4;
Matt. 18:21–22

1. What are we to do when we pray?
2. How many times should we forgive?

❧ *Prayer* ❧

Father, help me to realize that nothing anyone has ever done against me compares to what I have done against You. You have forgiven me – help me to forgive others. And not grudgingly, but graciously. In Jesus' Name. Amen.

Leave nothing behind

"We died to sin; how can we live in it any longer?" (v.2)

For reading & meditation – Romans 6:1–14

We look now at another thing we must do if we are to stay spiritually fresh – break decisively with everything of which Christ cannot approve. We have seen the importance of getting rid of grudges and resentments, but now we go a stage further and focus on getting rid of everything that mars our relationship with the Master. This means that we must make up our minds that anything the Lord speaks to us about must go. There is to be no trifling.

A gardener who works in an evangelical conference center tells how, during the first two or three days of a conference, Christians are keen to obey the signs that say, "Do not drop litter." They go out of their way to carry unwanted paper to the litter bins. After four or five days have passed, however, he finds that people get tired of looking for the bins and hide their unwanted paper under the bushes. They have enough conscience to hide the paper, but not enough to get rid of it.

Do not let this matter of getting rid of the things of which Christ disapproves end in a compromise or a stalemate. Look down into the hidden recesses where your sins may have been tucked away, and bring them all out – every one. They will plead to be left alone, but bring them all out – not a thing must be left behind. Don't be content with a conscience that will hide sins but not get rid of sins. If I had to put into one word the biggest single barrier to maintaining spiritual freshness, it would be this – procrastination. So be decisive – beginning today.

FURTHER STUDY

Acts 24:1–25;
Jer. 8:20;
Heb. 3:7–15

1. What was Felix's mistake?

2. What lesson must we learn from the children of Israel?

⊷ *Prayer* ⊷

Father, I have put my hand to the plow and I do not intend to look back. This shall be no halfway business. Help me to bring to You everything that needs to be dealt with today. In Jesus' Name. Amen.

Get on the offensive

"... if your hand causes you to sin, cut it off ..." (v.43)
For reading & meditation – Mark 9:38–50

W e continue meditating on the importance of breaking decisively with everything of which Christ cannot approve. Yesterday we discussed the problem of Christians who hide sins but are not willing to get rid of them. Let there be no illusion about this – no one can maintain their spiritual freshness as long as they allow known sin to remain and take root in their lives.

The matter of spiritual freshness is decided, not by living on the defensive but by living on the offensive. It involves making definite decisions – decisions such as saying "Yes" to all that Christ offers and saying "No" to all that sin offers. "Christianity," said someone, "is not a prohibition, but a privilege." I would agree with that, but would add that it does, however, have a prohibition in it. In our text for today, Jesus says that if your "hand" or your "eye" causes you to sin, then do something about it. In other words, do not tolerate anything that cuts across the central purpose of your life. From head to foot, you are to belong to Christ.

The order in these verses is important. The order is hand, foot, eye. The "hand" represents the doing of evil, the "foot" the approach toward evil, and the "eye" the seeing of evil with desire from afar. What's the message in all this? Quite clearly, the message is that sin must be cut out at every stage. The place to begin, of course, is with the "eye" – the place of desire. Take care of that and you won't have to worry too much about the "hand" and the "foot."

FURTHER STUDY

Matt. 16:21–27;
Luke 14:26–27;
Mark 10:28

1. What does it mean to "take up our cross"?

2. What was Peter's declaration?

◆━ *Prayer* ━◆

O Father, teach me how to be a decisive and not a double-minded person – especially in relation to this matter of sin. Show me what things I need to break with in my life and help me to do it. In Jesus' Name. Amen.

The best place to kill a cobra ...

"The eye is the lamp of the body. If your eyes are good, your whole body will be full of light." (v.22)

For reading & meditation – Matthew 6:19–34

We said yesterday that the most effective place to deal with sin is at the "eye" stage. That may mean the actual seeing of evil with the physical eye, or seeing it in imagination with the mental eye. "The best place to kill a cobra," runs an old Indian proverb, "is in its egg."

Most sin follows on from a failure to kill it at the place of desire – the "eye." When an evil thought comes, try blinking your eyes very rapidly and you will discover that the thought is broken up. It is a voluntary act demanding the attention of the will, and thus draws attention away from the evil thought. Add to the action the simple prayer that Peter prayed when he was about to sink into the waters of the Sea of Galilee: "Lord, save me."

Another thing you can do when a sinful thought or desire invades your mind is to change whatever you are doing in order to focus your attention elsewhere. An old Welsh miner I knew told me many years ago that when he was a young man, he was out walking one day and was attacked with an evil thought. He deliberately picked up a heavy stone and carried it back home. The attention necessary to carry the load made him forget the thought. These ideas may not work for everyone, but they have certainly worked for some. Another way to deal with an evil thought or desire when it comes is to focus your attention on a mental picture of Christ on the Cross. It is hard to think of evil and Him at the same time. They are incompatibilities.

FURTHER STUDY

Isa. 33:10–17;
Psa. 119:59;
Prov. 15:26;
Rom. 8:6

1. What is the result of refusing to contemplate evil?

2. How will you guard your eyes today?

⊷ *Prayer* ⊶

O Lord, help me to outmaneuver any sinful thoughts that come into my mind. Give me the kind of mind in which You can be at home. This I ask in Jesus' peerless and precious Name. Amen.

"Every sin can be overcome"

"Rather, clothe yourselves with the Lord Jesus Christ …" (v.14)

For reading & meditation – Romans 13:1–14

Every sin can be overcome. Don't allow yourself to admit to any exception, for if you do, that exception will be the loose bolt that causes the bridge to fall down.

One of the sad things about certain sections of the modern-day Church is the moral fatalism that says in regard to one's personal sin: "But what could I do? I am just a frail human being." The implication is that sin is an integral part of human nature, and as long as we remain human, we shall never be able to overcome sin. The clear message of the Gospel is spelled out in this verse: "Sin will have no dominion over you" (Rom. 6:14, RSV).

Today's text in the Amplified Bible reads: "But clothe yourself with the Lord Jesus Christ, the Messiah, and make no provision for indulging the flesh – put a stop to thinking about the evil cravings of your physical nature – to gratify its desires and lusts." Notice the phrase – "make no provision for indulging the flesh." In other words – do not provide for failure, provide for victory. There must be an absoluteness about the whole thing. There are dangers in pretending we are winning the battle against sin when we are not, or in approaching the whole issue from self-effort. But these dangers, in my opinion, are not as great as mentally providing for sin in our lives. The tyranny of the fatalism that as long as we are in the flesh, we must expect to sin, must be broken. The Christian life must be lived from the standpoint that we expect not to sin. I repeat: *every sin can be overcome.*

FURTHER STUDY

Rom. chs. 7 & 8; 6:11; John 8:34

1. What set Paul free?

2. What is the obligation we have?

⊷ *Prayer* ⊶

My Father and my God, help me to lay hold on the fact that Your offer is not simply to help me realize what sin is, but to release me from it. May I enter more and more into that glorious deliverance day by day. Amen.

"But your head is gone"

"Christ has utterly wiped out the damning evidence of broken laws ..."
(v.14, J. B. Phillips)

For reading & meditation – Colossians 2:6–19

We spend one more day focusing on the thought that one of the things we must do if we are to stay spiritually fresh is to break decisively with everything that Christ cannot approve.

When we are fighting sin and evil, we are fighting a defeated foe. Jesus met and conquered every sin on the Cross. You will never meet a single sin that has not been defeated by Christ. If sin is bullying you, do what E. Stanley Jones advised. He said: "When sin intimidates me, I quietly ask it to bend its neck. When it does, I joyfully point to the footprints of the Son of God on its neck. My inferiority complex is gone. I am on the winning side." The language may be picturesque but the truth is powerful – because of what Christ has accomplished on Calvary, we walk the earth amid conquered foes.

A far-fetched but illustrative story from the ancient battles of Africa tells how during a skirmish a warrior was beheaded, but he fought on even though his head was gone. He succeeded in killing many until someone said, "But your head has gone – you're dead," whereupon he fell down and died. When sin comes against you, point and say: "Look, your head has gone. My Master conquered you on the Cross. Begone! You are headless." Evil fights on but it is brainless. It depends on prejudices, old habits, and perhaps above all on our lack of decisiveness. So if there are still any sins in your life that need to be dealt with, face them in the assurance that they are conquered foes and break decisively with everything that Christ cannot approve.

FURTHER STUDY

1 John ch. 1;
Prov. 28:13;
Acts 3:19

1. What prevents us from prospering?

2. How are we to deal with sin?

✦ *Prayer* ✦

O God, thank You for reminding me that I need not develop an inferiority complex in relation to sin – it is a conquered foe. Help me to accept and enter into the great victory of Calvary. In Christ's powerful Name. Amen.

Our chief resource

"... be filled with the Spirit." (v.18)

For reading & meditation – Ephesians 5:15–27

W e continue meditating on the things we must do in order to maintain spiritual freshness. My next suggestion is this: daily open your being to the presence and power of the Holy Spirit.

A number of Christians I meet shrink from any talk of the Holy Spirit for fear they will be labelled "charismatic." People sometimes write to me and say: "We can't quite tell from your writings whether you are a charismatic or a non-charismatic. What line do you take as far as this is concerned?" My usual reply is that I refuse to wear any label other than that of a child of the living God. I know that whenever I talk about the Holy Spirit, I run the risk of alienating some of my audience who think that because of the overemphasis in some circles on matters relating to the third Person of the Trinity, it is best to avoid any mention of Him.

However, according to Scripture, the Holy Spirit is the chief resource for spiritual freshness. Unless we have a continuous encounter with Him, our lives will lack vitality and exuberance. I say "continuous encounter," because there are some Christians who think that because they have been filled with the Holy Spirit at some time in their past, that is enough. It is not. Our text for today tells us: "Ever be filled and stimulated with the Holy Spirit" (Amplified Bible). We need a constant replenishing of the resources of the Holy Spirit. As Billy Graham replied when someone asked why he said that he prayed to be continually filled with the Holy Spirit: "Because I leak."

FURTHER STUDY

Acts ch. 2; 1:8;
Joel 2:28

1. What did Jesus promise?

2. What was the result?

⋯⊷ *Prayer* ⊶⋯

Gracious Father, fill me with Your Spirit. Help me to know the experience of a daily infilling, a constant topping-up. Help me to be open to all Your resources, especially those that are supplied by Your Spirit. Amen.

What if...?

*"But you will receive power when the Holy Spirit comes on
you; and you will be my witnesses ..." (v.8)*

For reading & meditation – Acts 1:1–11

We said yesterday that the chief resource for maintaining spiritual freshness is the Holy Spirit. A little boy, when asked what the Holy Spirit means, replied: "I suppose it is what puts the 'oomph' into Christianity." He was on the right track, but failed to use the correct pronoun – not "it" but "He." The Holy Spirit is not an influence but a Person. This is why Scripture, when referring to Him, uses personal pronouns such as "He," "who" and "whom."

Suppose there had been no Holy Spirit? Then we would have been faced with a religion in which there was little "oomph." We would have the four Gospels without the Upper Room – distinctive, but not dynamic. Take Mark's Gospel, for example; if there had been no Day of Pentecost, the message of Christ would have ended with these words: "Then they went out and fled from the tomb, for trembling and bewilderment and consternation had seized them. And they said nothing about it to anyone, for they were held by alarm and fear" (Mark 16:8, Amplified Bible).

What a sad plight we would all be in if the message of Christ had ended there. The resurrection had taken place, the whole of the redemptive process was complete, the gladdest news that had ever burst upon human ears was in the possession of the disciples – but "they said nothing about it to anyone, for they were held by alarm and fear." If Christianity had ended there, it would not have been a gospel that conquered the world. No amount of good information could have transformed those early disciples. Something else was needed – the Holy Spirit.

FURTHER STUDY
John 16:1–16; 14:26;
15:26–27

1. What did Jesus say of
the Holy Spirit?

2. What is another title
of the Holy Spirit?

⤐ *Prayer* ⟜

O God, help me not to live in the twilight zone between Resurrection and Pentecost. I want to know all the fullness of the Upper Room in my life. Turn me from a flickering torch into a flaming torch. In Jesus' Name. Amen.

Dividing line of the centuries

"And they were all filled with the Holy Spirit and began to speak with other tongues ..." (v.4, NASB)

For reading & meditation – Acts 2:1–21

*W*e ended yesterday with the thought that it was the Holy Spirit who transformed the early disciples from timid and disconsolate men into men who were ablaze and invincible.

If you draw a line through the pages of the New Testament, you will find on one side a good deal of spiritual staleness, while on the other an abundance of spiritual freshness. That line runs straight through an Upper Room where a group of people waited in simple confidence for the promise their Master had made to them to be fulfilled. We read: "They were all filled with the Holy Spirit." That filling was the dividing line in the moral and spiritual development of humanity. It marked a new era – the era of the Holy Spirit.

On the other side of that dividing line, prior to Pentecost, the disciples were spasmodic in their allegiance and achievements. Sometimes they could rejoice that evil spirits were subject to them, and sometimes they had to ask, "Why could we not cast it out?" Sometimes they appeared ready to go to death with Jesus, and sometimes they quarrelled over who should have first place in His Kingdom. Simon Peter could whip out a sword and cut off the ear of the High Priest's servant, and then quail before the gaze of a serving maid. Then came Pentecost. A divine reinforcement took place. They were new men doing new work; no longer spasmodic, but stable. On which side of that dividing line are you? Are you a pre-Pentecost Christian, spasmodic and intermittent, or a post-Pentecost Christian – dynamic and different?

FURTHER STUDY

2 Cor. 3:1–6;
John 6:63;
Rom. 8:11;
1 Pet. 3:18

1. What does the letter of the Law do?

2. What changes this?

⇥ *Prayer* ⇤

O God, forgive me that so often I am crouching behind closed doors instead of being out on the open road. Make me a post-Pentecostal Christian. In Jesus' Name. Amen.

"Life unlimited"

*"He who believes in Me ... 'From his innermost being shall
flow rivers of living water.' " (v.38, NASB)*

For reading & meditation – John 7:25–39

*I*t is quite clear from the words before us today that the
followers of Christ are meant to have rivers of living water
flowing out of them. The Amplified Bible translates this
passage: "He who believes in Me ... From his innermost being
shall flow continuously springs and rivers of living water. But He
was speaking here of the Spirit, Whom those who believe in Him
were afterwards to receive."

Are our lives truly like this? Do fresh springs flow out of us day
after day? If not, why not? The answer is simple – there can be no
outflow unless there is an inflow. The rhythm of the life of the
Spirit is this – intake and outflow. If there is more intake than
outflow, then the intake stops; if there is more outflow than intake,
then the outflow stops. The doors open inward to receive, only to
open outward to give.

When we come to talk about life in the Spirit, we are not to
think in terms of a reservoir which has only limited resources. Life
is a channel, attached to infinite resources. The more we draw on
those resources, the more we have. There is no danger of
exhausting one's resources. We do not have to hold back, for the
more we give, the more we have. Living on the overflow is what
many of us lack today. A sign could be put up over our individual
and collective lives saying, "Life Limited." According to Jesus'
promise, when the Spirit comes, life is unlimited: "From your
innermost being shall flow rivers of living water." Not rivulets, not
trickles, not brooks, not streams – but rivers. Rivers!

FURTHER STUDY

Acts 10:34–38;
1 Cor. 3:16; 6:19;
2 Tim. 1:14

1. How did Peter link
Christ's work and the
ministry of the Holy
Spirit?

2. What has God made
us?

Prayer

*O God, take me from life limited to Life Unlimited. Help me to link my channel
to Your infinite resources. Flow through me until I become a flowing river; no,
rather an overflowing river. In Jesus' Name. Amen.*

The abiding Presence

*"... you know Him because He abides with you,
and will be in you." (v.17, NASB)*

For reading & meditation – John 14:15–27

There is an all-at-onceness about the coming of the Holy Spirit into our lives – and also a continuity.

Marriage is perhaps the best illustration I can use to clarify what I mean here. Just as there is an all-at-onceness about marriage – you don't get married again every day if you are really married; it is a once and for all – yet there are daily adjustments to be made around the great central adjustment. You can be married all at once, yet it takes a long time to be married well, for more and more mutual adjustments have to be made, and more and more areas of surrender experienced. "Surrender" is the initial word in any relationship – whether human or divine – and then other words come in, such as "gladly yielding" and "joyful response." As someone has put it: "I surrender to surrender. I yield to yielding and I respond to response."

The initial surrender to God brings, or should bring, an attitude of response to all of God's commands. And one of those commands, remember, is to be continuously filled with the Holy Spirit. As D. L. Moody once put it: "Ephesians 5:18 is not just an experience to be enjoyed but a command to be obeyed. If we do not open ourselves to a daily encounter with the Holy Spirit, the inevitable conclusion is that we are disobedient Christians."

One final word of advice – make sure, when you ask God to fill you daily with His Spirit, that you are not just looking for a momentary thrill or a passing influence that will pull you out of a spiritual "low." He wants to come in – to abide.

FURTHER STUDY

Acts 10:39–48;
Judges 6:34; 14:6;
1 Sam. 10:10; 16:13

1. List some of the O.T. saints who were anointed by the Holy Spirit.

2. What change did Pentecost make?

⇢ *Prayer* ⇠

O Father, forgive me that I tend to treat the Holy Spirit more as a Visitor than a Companion. From today on, I want that to change. Come in, Holy Spirit, to reside and preside. In Christ's Name I pray. Amen.

Not a trap – a temple

"... a body you prepared for me." (v.5)

For reading & meditation – Hebrews 10:1–10

We continue to meditate on things we must do if we are to stay spiritually fresh. My next suggestion may come as a surprise – keep your body in good physical shape.

One of the most disastrous divorces that ever took place in Christendom was that between the physical and the spiritual. In early Christianity, they were one. When the disciples wanted men to look after the physical nourishment of those who were in need in the early Church, the first of those they selected was Stephen, a man "full of faith and of the Holy Spirit" (Acts 6:5, NASB). Faith and the Holy Spirit were to be carried into the satisfying of physical needs, for the Early Church regarded the physical as being important, as well as the spiritual. Not supremely important, of course, but important nevertheless.

In more recent centuries of the Christian Church, the physical has been looked upon with great suspicion. In my youth I heard thundering sermons on the text, "our vile body" (Phil. 3:21, KJV), in which preachers propounded the idea that the body was the enemy of the soul. The suggestion was that the body must be ignored until the day when it is finally discarded and we are given a new resurrection body. These preachers failed to understand that the phrase "vile body" in the King James Version really means "body of humiliation," and not something to be treated with contempt. Let's have done with this morbid idea concerning the body which still lingers in parts of the Christian Church. Our bodies are not to be seen as traps, but as temples of the Holy Spirit.

FURTHER STUDY

Rom. 12:1–8; 6:13;
2 Cor. 6:16

1. What are we to offer God?

2. What are we to honor God with?

✦⇥ *Prayer* ⇤✦

Blessed Lord Jesus, help me see my body in the way You saw Yours – not as something to be avoided but as something to be used. Show me the steps I need to take to be healthy in soul and in body. For Your own dear Name's sake. Amen.

Body and soul - united

"... May your whole spirit, soul and body be kept blameless at the coming of our Lord Jesus Christ." (v.23)

For reading & meditation – 1 Thessalonians 5:12–24

We saw yesterday how centuries of misunderstanding have brought about a division between the body and the soul. And this division is in evidence in some parts of the Church today. Jesus, however, did not see His body as something to be ignored, but as something to be used. "You have made ready a body for Me to offer" (Heb. 10:5, Amplified Bible). His body and soul were attuned. He neither neglected His body nor pampered it, but offered it as the vehicle of God's will and purpose. And He kept it fit for God. There is no mention of His ever being sick. Tired, yes – but never ill. It is an accepted fact today that body and soul are a unity, and that a sick soul can produce a sick body.

A healthy spirit contributes to a healthy body. However, it works the other way around – a healthy body can contribute to good emotional and mental health. We Christians tend to overemphasize the spiritual side of life and underestimate the importance of physical facts like body chemistry, weather, water, air pollution and nutrition.

Through ignorance of the way in which body and soul are related, we succeed in tearing them apart. What is said about husband and wife in the marriage service can also be applied to the body and the soul: "What therefore God has joined together, let not man put asunder" (Matt. 19:6, RSV). A good pianist may be able to get a lot out of a poor instrument, but he cannot give full expression to the music if the piano is out of tune. You cannot ignore the physical if you want to stay spiritually fresh.

FURTHER STUDY

1 Kings ch. 19;
Rom. 8:11;
1 Cor. 3:16

1. What was part of Elijah's problem?

2. How did the angel minister to Elijah?

⇒ *Prayer* ⇐

O Father, help me see that my body is not something over which to be offended, but something to be offered. Give me a balanced understanding of this matter so that I can be at my best for You – spirit, soul and body. Amen.

Suicide's most deadly weapons

*"So whether you eat or drink or whatever you do,
do it all for the glory of God." (v.31)*

For reading & meditation – 1 Corinthians 10:23–33

*D*isregard of the physical aspect of life can greatly contribute to spiritual dryness. This means that a certain amount of discipline must be introduced into our lives. But what kind of discipline?

Firstly, discipline in what and how much we eat. Every meal should be a sacrament offered on the altar of fitter and finer living. Doctors tell us that excess food – as well as too little food – destroys brain power. What is in the stomach often determines what is in the head. Scripture says: "... for the kingdom of God is not food and drink" (Rom. 14:17, NKJV), but it is not a contradiction of that verse to say that often our food and drink determine our fitness for the kingdom of God.

Seneca, in an exaggerated statement made for the sake of emphasis, said: "Man does not die: he kills himself." Dr. R. L. Greene, a professor of chemistry and a specialist in nutrition, says: "The most deadly weapons used by man in committing suicide are the knife, fork and spoon." You may be repelled at the idea of committing suicide – and so you should be – but you may well be contributing to your death by wrong ways of eating.

We need discipline also to ensure that we get at least the minimum amount of vitamins. Vitamins are necessary to vitality; they are God's gift to us. The divine Chemist has designed our bodies to work in a certain way, and if we ignore His prescription, we reduce our physical effectiveness. And reducing physical effectiveness can also reduce spiritual effectiveness.

FURTHER STUDY

Prov. 23:1–21;
Eccl. 6:7;
Phil. 3:19

1. How does the Scripture regard gluttony?

2. What is gluttony?

⟶ *Prayer* ⟵

O Father, help me to recognize that physical vitality contributes to spiritual vitality. May I respect the body You have given me and pay attention to the laws of health that You have built into the universe. In Jesus' Name I pray. Amen.

The body – a fine-tuned violin

*"So he got up and ate and drank. Strengthened by that food ...
forty days and forty nights ..." (v.8)*

For reading & meditation – 1 Kings 19:1–8

We saw yesterday that what and how much we eat can greatly affect the way we feel. If the nerves are starved on account of a lack of vitamins, they will kick back in physical depression in exactly the same way that a starved soul or spirit will kick back in psychological depression. So discipline yourself to eat correctly and nutritionally.

Next, discipline yourself to take appropriate physical exercise. God designed our bodies for movement and if they don't move, they get sluggish. Then what happens? A sluggish body contributes to a sluggish spirit. Time and time again, when counselling people with depression, along with other suggestions, I have recommended them to take up physical exercise. One should not, of course, embark upon vigorous exercise like playing squash or jogging without having a medical check-up, but I have been surprised at how even a short, brisk walk can do wonders for the soul.

I feel a word of caution may be needed here as we are passing through a stage in our culture when people are fast becoming exercise "freaks." It is possible to regulate the body too much. You should get enough exercise to remain fit but also keep in mind that too much attention to exercise or sports may drain higher interests. Everything must be kept in balance: just enough food to keep you fit and not enough to make you fat; just enough sleep to keep you fresh and a little less than that which would make you lazy. We must keep our bodies like a fine-tuned violin and then the music of God will come out from every fiber of our being.

FURTHER STUDY

Phil. 3:1–16;
1 Cor. 9:24;
Gal. 2:2;
Heb. 12:1

1. What picture did Paul use in illustrating truth?

2. How much exercise do you take?

⊷ *Prayer* ⊷

O God of my mind and my body, I come to You to have both brought under the control of Your redemption and Your guidance. May I pass on the health of my mind to my body and the health of my body to my mind. Amen.

Be selective

"... he said to them, 'Come with me by yourselves to a quiet place and get some rest.'" (v.31)

For reading & meditation – Mark 6:30–44

*W*e have been saying over these past few days that disregard of our physical life may affect our spiritual well-being, for what goes on in the body greatly influences, though it does not control, what goes on in the soul and spirit.

My third suggestion in relation to this physical aspect of our lives is this – discipline your times of rest and recreation. Some recreations do not recreate – they exhaust one. They leave one morally and spiritually flabby and unfit. I find that after watching some television programs I have been challenged or lifted, but others leave me feeling inwardly ravished. The delicacies of life seem somehow to have been invaded, the finest flowers of the spirit trampled on and one comes out drooping. I am learning to be more selective in my recreations. One should never expose oneself to a film or television program that is likely to leave one spiritually or morally depleted – not if you value the higher values. It is like allowing pigs into your parlor.

The same can be said of other recreations. Some pieces of literature can leave you with a sense of moral and spiritual exhaustion. Don't fall for the idea that one has to read everything that comes to hand in order to understand life. This is where many of our Christian young people need help. Does one have to wallow in a mud-hole in order to understand filth? Does a doctor have to take germs into his own body in order to understand how they function? Recreation is extremely important to help us stay spiritually fresh, but we need to make sure our recreations really recreate.

FURTHER STUDY

Heb. 4:1–11;
Ex. 33:14;
Matt. 11:29

1. What are we invited to enter into?

2. What does this mean in practical terms?

⊷ *Prayer* ⊶

Father, You have made me for health and rhythm. Help me to be sensitive to all the things I need to do so that I am at my best spiritually and physically. I want to honor You in everything I do – even my recreations. Amen.

Taking every project prisoner

" ... I take every project prisoner to make it obey Christ."
(v.5, Moffatt)

For reading & meditation – 2 Corinthians 10:1–14

We continue looking at things we can do to stay spiritually fresh. Another suggestion is this – learn how to deal with frustration. Time and time again, I have sat with people who have said: "What's wrong with me? I feel so low spiritually. I am not involved in sin. Why does my Christian life feel so stale?" On many of those occasions, I have observed that the problem contributing to their feelings of spiritual staleness is an inability to cope with frustration.

One of the most radiant Christians I have ever met was a seed salesman in West Wales whose name was Mordecai Price. Crippled in both his lower limbs by poliomyelitis, he drove a hand-controlled car and would make his way to outlying farms to sell seed to the farmers. Sometimes it would take him an hour just to get out of his car and open a farm gate – but he persevered nevertheless.

One day I said to him: "Don't you get frustrated by your condition? How do you keep going like this when many others would have settled for a lifetime of invalidism and inactivity?" He has gone to be with the Lord now, but his reply has lived on in my heart for over thirty years: "I take every project prisoner to make it obey Christ – even the project of poliomyelitis." He had learned how to make his frustration fruitful. When you and I can learn how to turn the ugly into the beautiful, the evil into the good, then frustration will never get a hold on us. The secret of living is the secret of using. Learn that and you will never be frustrated again.

FURTHER STUDY

2 Cor. 4:1–10;
Psa. 44:5;
Rom. 8:35–37

1. What was Paul's testimony?

2. What does it mean to be "more than a conqueror"?

⊷❖ *Prayer* ❖⊶

O Father, teach me how to turn the ugly into the beautiful, the evil into the good and take every project prisoner for Christ. I ask this for Your own dear Name's sake. Amen.

What is frustration?

*"If I must boast, I will boast of the things that
show my weakness." (v.30)*

For reading & meditation – 2 Corinthians 11:16–30

We said yesterday that one of the biggest contributors to spiritual staleness is frustration. But what is frustration? The dictionary defines it as "being baffled, balked, neutralized, disappointed." Is there a strategy that will enable us to deal effectively with such things so that we can stay spiritually fresh.

When I left college and went into the ministry, I came up against so many problems that I became increasingly frustrated. I knew all the theory of staying on top spiritually – get rid of sin, pray and read the Bible every day, praise the Lord in all things, see everything that happens from His point of view, and so on. The theory I had learned in theological college, however, just didn't seem to work in everyday life. In fact, looking back on those early years, I think I had learned most of the secrets of effective Christian living except how to overcome frustration. I remember crying out to God day after day: "O Lord, show me how to avoid being frustrated."

The secret was taught to me by a radiant Christian woman whose life was filled with more potentially frustrating situations than anyone I have ever known. In fact, I said to her one day: "You seem to be a target for everyone. How do you manage to stay so spiritually alive and alert in all this?" She said: "All my days are happy, even when everyone hits the bull's eye. I heal as quickly as they pull the trigger." I said: "Teach me the secrets of responding like this." She did, and over the next few days I will share them with you.

FURTHER STUDY

Acts 16:1–10;
Phil. 4:11–12;
1 Tim. 6:6

1. What was a key in Paul's life?

2. How did he overcome frustrating circumstances?

⊷ *Prayer* ⊷

Father, You have taught me many secrets – teach me this one also. Show me how to take whatever comes and turn it to good. Give me a spirit that bends without breaking. In Jesus' Name I pray. Amen.

The lyre pine

"... He causes his sun to rise on the evil and the good, and sends rain on the righteous and the unrighteous." (v.45)

For reading & meditation – Matthew 5:38–48

I ended yesterday with the promise that I would share with you the lessons taught me by a radiant Christian woman on how to overcome frustration. In case of doubt, let me make clear that the woman concerned was not a thick-skinned individual who cared for nothing and nobody, but a highly sensitive person who knew how to turn every test into a testimony.

Here is her prescription for overcoming frustration. Firstly, realize that Christians aren't exempt from facing problems. It is true that Christians are exempted from many self-inflicted pains which non-Christians bring on themselves through wrong attitudes, wrong moral choices, wrong behavior and so on. But this apart, every Christian is as subject as a non-Christian to accidents, sickness and even death. Some years ago a plane full of non-Christian Indian seamen crashed into the Alps; a few days later, fifty-eight Christians, fresh from a conference, crashed in the same Alps.

Secondly, fix in your mind that the Christian answer is along the line of using whatever comes – justice or injustice, pain or pleasure, compliment or criticism. Ever heard of a lyre pine? The lyre pine is a pine tree whose top is shaped like a lyre (harp) with a number of branches forming the top, instead of one straight branch. It is produced, they say, by a calamity such as a storm or a lightning flash striking off the original top. Frustrated, it then puts up a whole series of tops stretched on a more or less horizontal bar. This can happen to us – if we let it. Calamity can turn dullness into music, a lone top into a lyre.

FURTHER STUDY

1 Pet. 1:1–7; 4:12–13;
John 16:33;
2 Cor. 4:17;
Rom. 5:3

1. What is the sequence of God's dealings in our lives?

2. How is this working out in your life?

⊷ *Prayer* ⊷ ——

Father, let this truth sink deeply into my spirit so that I will be able to turn all my lone tops into lyres. Quicken within me today the sense that with You, I can overcome everything – including frustration. Amen.

Making every sadness sing

"But he gives us more grace ..." (v.6)

For reading & meditation – James 4:1–10

We continue with our prescription for overcoming frustration. Thirdly, expect God to supply you with the strength to transform everything that comes to make it contribute to the central purposes for which you live.

"Expect God to supply you with strength." That is the secret – in the Christian life, we get what we expect. You must have heard the story of the woman who, having heard a sermon on the text: "Whosoever shall say unto this mountain, Be thou removed," decided to try out her faith on a mountain near her home. Prior to going to sleep, she looked out of her window and said to the mountain, "Be thou removed." In the morning, as soon as she awoke, she looked out, saw that the mountain was still there and said woefully: "Just as I expected." In the Christian life, we get what we expect.

Notice the rest of the phrase: "... strength to transform everything that comes ..." This is what Jesus did. Luke says: "And He was withdrawn from them about a stone's throw, and He knelt down and prayed, saying 'Father, if it is Your will, take this cup away from Me; nevertheless not My will, but Yours, be done.' Then an angel appeared to Him from heaven, strengthening Him" (Luke 22:41–43, NKJV). Here, God's answer was not to take away the cup, but to supply strength to make that bitter cup into a cup of salvation which He would put to the thirsty lips of humanity. God's answer was strength to use, not exemption from. In the midst of your trials, don't whine to be released; ask rather for strength to make every sadness sing.

FURTHER STUDY

Isa. ch. 40; 41:10;
2 Cor. 12:9

1. What is promised to those who wait on the Lord?

2. What was Paul's testimony?

⊷ *Prayer* ⊷

Father, don't ever let me forget this lesson – that if I cannot change my surroundings, I can change my soul. Help me see that if I am not saved from a situation, then I can be saved in the situation. I am deeply thankful. Amen.

Positive thanksgiving

"Let the peace of Christ rule in your hearts ... And be thankful." (v.15)

For reading & meditation – Colossians 3:12–25

We spend one more day looking at a prescription for overcoming frustration. Fourthly, look for something good to come out of everything that appears bad. How I wish I could hammer this thought into the mind of every Christian.

Nowadays, it is almost second nature with me to look for a positive in every negative – but it was not always so. At one time, whenever anything bad happened to me, I used to say: "Oh no, not again. Just when everything seemed to be going right. Why should this happen to me?" I learned, however, to apply the principle of looking for good in everything bad, and I can honestly say it has transformed my whole life and ministry. It means also learning to thank God for the good that is emerging, instead of brooding over any loss that has been sustained. The positive thanksgiving will make your heart receptive to God's power. He can do anything with a thankful heart, but He can do little or nothing for a complaining, self-pitying heart. It is closed to grace.

Fifthly and finally, find someone who is going through difficult circumstances and help them find victory. Someone has said, "Sorrow expands the soul for joy." For joy? Yes – the joy of being useful and creative. God uses frustrating circumstances to prune you for fruit-bearing. The lessons you have learned will go even deeper as you share them with others. Expression deepens impression. If you syndicate your sorrows, they will multiply. If you syndicate your blessings, they will multiply. Learn this secret and it will help you stay spiritually on top – no matter what.

FURTHER STUDY

Rom. 8:1–7;
Psa. 29:11;
Phil. 4:7

1. What brings life and peace?

2. What will the peace of God do?

⤞ *Prayer* ⤝

O God, help me not to be a whiner, but a worshiper. Help me to cultivate an attitude of thanksgiving in all things – for all things serve. I ask this in and through the peerless and precious Name of Jesus. Amen.

Experience ... expression

"They asked each other, 'Were not our hearts burning within us ...?' Then the two told what happened ..." (vv.32 & 35)

For reading & meditation – Luke 24:13–35

We turn now to look at yet another thing we can do to stay spiritually fresh – take time to share with others the things that God has shared with us. Is the Christian life a kind of secret society between God and me? A solitary thing which I share with no one else? Of course not. It is a law of the spiritual life that that which is not expressed soon dies.

The great Bible expositor, Campbell Morgan, said: "There are two ways to kill the ministry of a preacher; one is to kill his experience of God and the other is to kill his expression of God." If his experience of God dies, then the effect of that central deadness will spread through all his work. It is like a stream without a source, or an effect without a cause. This is why Paul said to Timothy: "Take heed to yourself and to your teaching" (1 Tim. 4:16, RSV). First to "yourself" and then to your "teaching." Paul said something similar to the Ephesian elders: "Take heed to yourselves and to all the flock" (Acts 20:28, RSV).

But if killing a preacher's experience of God dries up his ministry, it is also true that killing his expression of God can have the same result. A minister who is restricted or restrained from sharing what God has shown him is like a stream that is blocked. He must find some way of getting through or else he will explode. And what is true of a preacher is true of every Christian. Experience – the intake – and expression – the outflow – are the alternate beats of the true Christian heart.

FURTHER STUDY

Phil. 2:1–13;
Matt. 10:32;
Luke 12:8

1. What are we to do?
2. Who will you share something with today?

❧ *Prayer* ❧

Father, I see that if either of these two things – experience and expression – grow faint within me, then I will lack spiritual vigor and vitality. Help me to maintain a healthy heartbeat – today and every day. Amen.

When God's people share

"We are therefore Christ's ambassadors, as though God were making his appeal through us ..." (v.20)

For reading & meditation – 2 Corinthians 5:11–21

W e looked yesterday at two important aspects of the Christian life – experience and expression. Both of these aspects are extremely important: if experience gets low, then expression gets low; if expression gets low, then experience gets low. We focus now on expression. If this side of the Christian life is not transformed from a bottled-up, non-contagious type of outflowing, then spiritual staleness is the inevitable result.

Two young men, both fairly new converts, had been listening to a sermon on evangelism. Afterwards, they approached their pastor and said: "We have never shared with anyone the experience we have had in Christ – how do we do it?" He suggested that they could go out, knock on a few doors and just begin to share their experience of Christ. The next night, in fear and trembling, they knocked on the first door of the street which they had decided to evangelize, and found it to be the home of a well-known lawyer. They were a little nonplussed when they discovered this, and blurted out: "We have come to invite you to join our church." The lawyer said: "A lot of people have asked me to join the church over the years – haven't you anything better than that to say to me?" They said: "Well, how about committing your life to Jesus Christ?" The lawyer invited them in, and within an hour had surrendered to Christ. "Now where do you go next," he said, "because I want to go with you." Before the end of the evening, the lawyer had the joy of witnessing another conversion like his own. Things happen when people share.

FURTHER STUDY

Acts ch. 2; 5:20; 18:9; 22:15

1. What was the hallmark of the early Church?

2. Witness to someone today.

⇥ *Prayer* ⇤

O Father, help me to come to such a place in my Christian life that in every situation where You want someone to pass on a special word from You, You will hear me say, "Here am I, Lord – send me." Amen.

"Anyone saved here lately?"

"... I always pray with joy because of your partnership in the gospel from the first day until now ..." (vv.4–5)

For reading & meditation – Philippians 1:1–11

e continue meditating on the importance of sharing with others what God has shared with us. Christianity is not merely a conception, but a contagion. And when the contagion is lost, the possibility is that the conception may be lost.

An American pastor, an old friend of mine, says: "Christianity is catching, and if people are not catching it from us, then perhaps it's because we do not have a sufficiently virulent case of it." Once, when he was in England we visited Westminster Abbey. He looked around and asked in loud tones: "Has anyone been saved here lately?" I said I was not sure, to which he replied: "If a church is not evangelistic, then it is not evangelical." He was right – but that didn't stop me from getting him outside as quickly as possible.

"Nothing is really ours," said C.S. Lewis, "until we share it." For the moment someone else shares our experience of Christ, then the faith means something more to us. The Amplified Bible translates the text before us today thus: "I thank my God for your fellowship – your sympathetic cooperation and contributions and partnership – in advancing the good news from the first day you heard it." From the very first day they stepped into the Kingdom of God, they began to contribute to it – to spread it. It was not something they learned – it was instinctive. It was as natural as a baby's cry at birth. Sharing Christ with others is not something we can take or leave; it is something which, if we don't take, we can easily lose. For the expression of the faith is the essence of the faith.

FURTHER STUDY

Mark 5:15–20;
Acts 1:8;
2 Tim. 1:8

1. What did Jesus tell the man to do?

2. What was Paul's admonition to Timothy?

✦ *Prayer* ✦

O Father, help us to be like the converts in the church at Philippi who, from the moment they saw You, wanted to share You. This we ask in Christ's precious and powerful Name. Amen.

The four words of the Gospel

"... the woman ... said to the people, 'Come, see a man who told me everything I ever did ...' "(vv.28–29)

For reading & meditation – John 4:27–42

We ended yesterday with the thought that in the true Christian heart, sharing is instinctive. What was the instinct of the woman at the well as soon as she had found salvation? It was to share what she had found with others.

What I am saying will cause some people to feel guilty, especially those who do not find it easy to share their faith. It is not that we should go out and accost everyone we meet with the message of salvation, but that we need to be alert for every opportunity and take advantage of it. The four words making up the Gospel and which are found in the passage before us today are "come ... see ... go ... tell." We get a first-hand knowledge – "come and see" – and then the instinctive impulse takes over – "go and tell." And if there is no "go and tell" impulse, then perhaps the "come and see" impulse is not ours – or it has ceased to hold a commanding place in our lives.

A woman once wrote to me following something I had written in *Every Day with Jesus* and said: "I had a real experience of God and refused to share it with anyone, so it died." How sad. J. B. Phillips' translation of 2 Corinthians 9:10 is luminous: "He who gives the seed to the sower ..." See the inference – He gives seed only to the one who uses it – the sower. If we won't use the seed, then we won't get it. Our powers are either dead or dedicated. If they are dedicated, they are alive with God. If they are saved up or conserved, they die.

FURTHER STUDY

1 Pet. 3:1–16;
Psa. 66:16;
Isa. 63:7

1. What must we always be prepared to do?

2. How did Isaiah and the psalmist do this?

⇢ *Prayer* ⇠

O Father, I ask not for an experience of You – that I already have. I ask rather for the courage to share it with others. Give me some seed today – and help me to sow it in prepared hearts. For Your own dear Name's sake. Amen.

"Let me commend my Savior"

"Then those who feared the Lord talked often one to another ..."
(v.16, Amplified Bible)

For reading & meditation – Malachi 3:1–18

We come back now to what we said on the first day of this particular section dealing with the importance of sharing Christ with others: experience and expression are the alternate beats of the Christian heart. And if these two things are not in operation, the Christian heart ceases to beat. Then what happens? We settle down to dead forms, dead attitudes and dead prayers.

This matter of sharing, however, must not be limited only to evangelism – it applies also to sharing with other Christians the things that God has shared with us. If God has shown you something today from His Word, then it is imperative that you share it with another Christian. As we have been saying, nothing is really ours until we share it – the expression will deepen the impression. So in seeking to stay spiritually fresh, discipline yourself to share appropriate issues with your Christian and non-Christian friends. Many do not do this. They are disciplined in their quiet time or their study of the Scriptures, but they have never disciplined themselves to share. Someone has defined a Christian as one who says by word or deed: "Let me commend my Savior to you." There is no better definition.

In a newspaper I saw a cartoon which showed a woman putting a garment around the shivering body of a little girl. Behind the woman stood Christ throwing a cloak around her shoulders. The title of the cartoon was this: "A proven assembly line." It is indeed a "proven assembly line." Give out to others and it will be given to you – pressed down and running over. Especially running over.

FURTHER STUDY

Jer. 20:1–9;
Acts 4:20;
2 Cor. 4:13

1. What was Jeremiah's confession?

2. What does believing produce?

⤙ *Prayer* ⤚

Father, I reach up to You with one hand and reach out to those in need with the other. Give me some word or message to pass on to a non-Christian or one of my Christian brothers or sisters this day. In Jesus' Name. Amen.

Fellowship

"And our fellowship is with the Father and with his Son, Jesus Christ." (v.3)

For reading & meditation – 1 John 1:1–10

Another suggestion to help us stay spiritually fresh is fellowship with other Christians. Daniel Rowlands, a famous Welsh revivalist of a past century, said: "The whole purpose of the Christian message can be summarized in a single word – fellowship."

What did he mean? Today's text spells it out clearly. Listen to it as it appears in the Amplified Bible: "What we have seen and heard, we are also telling you, so that you too may realize and enjoy fellowship as partners and partakers with us. And this fellowship that we have ... is with the Father and with His Son Jesus Christ, the Messiah." First of all, John seems to say that the fellowship is "with us," but he hastens to add that our fellowship "is with the Father and with His Son, Jesus Christ."

Follow me carefully now, for what I am about to say can be easily misunderstood: the person who does not know fellowship with God can never know fellowship with anyone else. It must be noted, of course, that I am here using the word "fellowship" in its highest possible sense. The one who does not know fellowship with God will feel, consciously or unconsciously, that he is cut off from the very roots of his being; he will feel like a spiritual orphan. This is why our horizontal relationships, that is, our relationship with ourselves and with others, can never be fully realized until we experience a vertical relationship – a relationship with God. When we are reconciled with God – and only then – do we have the potential for experiencing true fellowship with ourselves and with others.

FURTHER STUDY

Ex. 19:1–22; 20:21; 24:2; 25:22; 33:9

1. What was the key to Moses' ministry?

2. What was the effect?

⊷ Prayer ⊶

Father, I see that I cannot experience true fellowship with myself or others until I have known it with You. Help me to deepen my fellowship with You so that I might deepen it with others. In Jesus' Name. Amen.

The heartbeat of the universe

"They devoted themselves to the apostles' teaching and to the fellowship ..." (v.42)

For reading & meditation – Acts 2:37–47

e saw yesterday that in the highest sense of the word, fellowship with others is only possible as we experience fellowship with God. I read a passage in a book that said: "We can only get to know ourselves and others to the extent that we tune in to the heartbeat of the universe."

Here is a psychologist, a non-Christian, attempting to put into words one of the greatest truths of Scripture, namely that it is only as we have fellowship with God that we can experience fellowship with ourselves and others. What a pity he could not see that what he calls "the heartbeat of the universe" is the heart that was broken on the Cross. Isn't it sad that so many philosophers and scientists come so close to seeing the reality that lies behind the universe and yet, for some reason, side-step the great issue of entering into a personal relationship with God? They struggle to know the secrets of the cosmos, and yet miss the "open secret" of God's revelation through Christ which He laid bare at Calvary. Instead, they try to achieve fellowship through psychological processes that leave the heart estranged.

The astonishing rise in our day of the "group therapy movement" testifies to the need of the human heart for fellowship. Almost every country in the world reports a rapid rise of small groups meeting together to encourage, confront and stimulate one another toward good emotional health and maturity. The world is waking up to the fact that we are made for fellowship. Oh, if only they could see that fellowship which does not begin with God, does not begin.

FURTHER STUDY

1 John 1:1–7;
Rom. 1:11–12; 12:5

1. What is the purpose of fellowship?

2. Who do you have fellowship with?

✦ Prayer ✦

Father, I am so thankful for the discovery that fellowship cannot be produced by trying, but by trusting. It begins and ends with You. Take me deeper into Your heart that I might take others deeper into mine. For Jesus' sake. Amen.

Through a hole in the roof

"... For anyone who does not love his brother, whom he has seen, cannot love God, whom he has not seen." (v.20)

For reading & meditation – 1 John 4:7–21

The experience we gain in fellowshipping with other Christians ends in a deepening of our fellowship with God.

This truth was first brought home to me by Norman Grubb, the then Director of the Worldwide Evangelistic Crusade, an organization for which I have the highest regard. I once heard him say: "Imagine that at your birth, you were placed in a house with no doors and windows, and by some miracle you were able to survive and grow into an adult. For twenty years or so, you have not known anyone except yourself. Then one day, God blasts a hole in the roof and reveals Himself to you. You experience daily contact with God through that hole in the roof, and day by day you get to know Him better. Suddenly, for the first time in your life, you hear voices outside your house, voices of people like yourself. You long to make contact with them, but you can't get out because there are no doors and windows. However, as you lean against the walls of the house, you become aware that they are fairly thin; one big push and the walls fall outward. As the walls fall down, so does the roof, and assuming that you escape injury, you move forward to greet the people whose voices you have heard but never seen."

"Now," said Norman Grubb, "when the walls came down, so did the roof. This means that your contact with God is no longer restricted to a hole in the roof – the sky's the limit. The effort we make to fellowship with others results in an even greater awareness and understanding of God."

FURTHER STUDY

1 Pet. 3:1–8;
1 Cor. 1:10;
Eph. 4:3

1. What five things did Peter underline for good fellowship?

2. What are we to make every effort to do?

⇢ *Prayer* ⇠

O Father, can this really be true? Can I know You better because I know my brother better? Your Word suggests so. Help me understand it more clearly. In Jesus' Name I pray. Amen.

Touching the intangible

*"On that day you will realize that I am in my Father,
and you are in me, and I am in you." (v.20)*

For reading & meditation – John 14:1–21

We ended yesterday by saying that the effort we make to go outside of ourselves and relate to others results in a wider awareness and a deeper understanding of God. This has been one of the greatest and most exciting discoveries of my life. The more I have given myself to my brothers and sisters in Christ, the greater has been my awareness and understanding of God.

I am not saying that in order to know God, we first have to get to know each other – that would be blatant error. We can know about Him through such means as creation, providence and so on, but we can only know Him through His Son Jesus Christ. "No one has seen God at any time. The only begotten Son, who is in the bosom of the Father, He has declared Him" (John 1:18, NKJV). However, once we know Him in this way, our fellowship with Him and our understanding of Him can be deepened by our relationship with others who know Him.

How does this work? The more I have focused on learning to listen – really listen – to my brothers and sisters in Christ, the more I have found that the effort I have made to do this has resulted in a heightening of my ability to listen to God. And the more I have sought to understand the mystery of His dealings in their lives, the more I have come to know the depth and beauty of His character. Although, down the years, I have come to know Him intimately in prayer, I believe I can say that I know Him even better because I have met Him in others.

FURTHER STUDY

Gal. 2:1–20;
Col. 1:27;
1 John 3:24

1. How does God make His riches known?

2. Are those riches being made known to others through you?

⊷ *Prayer* ⊷

O Father, how can I sufficiently thank You for the fellowship we have with one another in Christ. In the tangible I see the Intangible, and through the visible I see the Invisible. I am eternally grateful. Amen.

The measure of maturity

*"... we saw a man driving out demons in your name and we
tried to stop him, because he is not one of us." (v.49)*

For reading & meditation – Luke 9:46–56

We spend one last day thinking through this important issue of how our fellowship with other Christians heightens our understanding of God and helps us stay spiritually fresh. I have no doubt that my fellowship with other Christians has helped more than words can convey to keep me spiritually alert and topped up. When, for some reason, I am not able to fellowship with other Christians, my spiritual life tends to sag. This is one of the laws of the Christian life and we ignore it to our peril.

Dr. E. Stanley Jones, said, "The measure of our spiritual maturity can be and is measured by the breadth and depth of our capacity and willingness for fellowship." Note the words "capacity" and "willingness." It doesn't mean working at enlarging our circle of fellowship – though for some it may mean that – but that we have the capacity and willingness to do it if God should so lead.

I know there are Christians in churches, fellowships and denominations whom I will never meet down here on earth, but I have the capacity and willingness to fellowship with them if God were to make it possible. We are as mature as our willingness and capacity for fellowship. In other words, if we cannot or do not want to fellowship with others who are truly Christ's, then we are immature Christians. Churches and denominations have different rules and guidelines in relation to mixing with others of different groups, but as far as individual fellowship is concerned, our basis ought to be this – everyone who belongs to Christ belongs to everyone else who belongs to Christ.

FURTHER STUDY

John 13:31–35;
Rom. 12:5;
1 Cor. 10:17;
Gal. 3:28

1. What is the greatest testimony to the world of Christ?

2. To what does Paul liken the body of Christ?

⊷ *Prayer* ⊷

Father, I see that if I shut out my brother, I shut out You – and my life will soon become stale. Help me deepen all the areas of my fellowship – my fellowship with You and my fellowship with others. In Jesus' Name. Amen.

The great Stimulator

"So by all the stimulus of Christ ..." (v.1, Moffatt)

For reading & meditation – Philippians 2:1–11

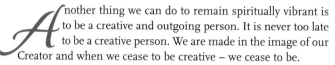

Another thing we can do to remain spiritually vibrant is to be a creative and outgoing person. It is never too late to be a creative person. We are made in the image of our Creator and when we cease to be creative – we cease to be.

Kagawa, the famous Japanese Christian, used to refer to Jesus as "the great Stimulator." One day some students asked him why he was so fond of this phrase, and he replied: "Because He stimulates the creative center in each one of us, making us first aware of God, and then aware of the infinite possibilities in God." When I was at school, I struggled a good deal with my studies, and although I passed all my examinations and went to college, my passes were always on the borderline. Then I found Christ as the great Stimulator – and what a change. He stimulated the creative center within me and so transformed my attitude to work that within months, I moved from near bottom of my classes to near the top.

When taking a seminar in Birmingham, I met a friend who had recently come to live there. "What do you think of Birmingham?" I said. His reply was a classic: "I have lived here for three months," he said, "and every day I keep seeing new horizons." This is what happens when we stay close to Jesus – every day we keep seeing new horizons. In His company we begin to see farther, feel for people on a wider scale, act more decisively, and live on the growing edge of adventure. Why? Because a creative God gives to His creation the same creative impulses.

FURTHER STUDY

John 1:1–18;
1 Cor. 8:6;
Col. 1:16

1. Who is at the center of creation?

2. What happens if He is the center of our lives?

✦ Prayer ✦

O God, stimulate my whole being, I pray, so that every day I shall see new horizons. Help me never to walk with my eyes focused on the ground, but with my eyes fixed on You. For Your own dear Name's sake I ask it. Amen.

Make the commonplace creative

"... They chose Stephen, a man full of faith and of the Holy Spirit; also Philip ..." (v.5)

For reading & meditation – Acts 6:1–8

We continue meditating on the importance of being a creative and outgoing person. No matter what happens to you, or when it happens to you, it is never too late to become creative. Pray, as one man did who was on the verge of going insane: "O Jesus, come into my soul, my mind, my body, into every brain cell and help me to be a contributive person." Jesus did come into every brain cell, and that man is now well and contributing to the Kingdom of God in an astonishing way.

I wonder, am I talking today to someone who feels they are caught up in so many routines that they are in a rut? Routines often become, if I might coin a word – *rut-ines*. They can make us into grooved, non-creative individuals, unless – and this is the point – unless we make the commonplace a creative place. And how do we do that? By the creative spirit we bring to it.

Someone has described Philip the evangelist as "a third-rate man in a second-rate task who did a first-rate job." He was quite different from the Philip who was one of Christ's original group of twelve disciples – he didn't have the privilege of having been chosen to be one of the apostolic band. He was one of "the seven" – whose task was "to wait on tables." He might have folded up under those limitations and said: "I am in a rut." Instead, however, he accepted the commonplace as a consecrated place and gently pushed against the barriers until they broke. His creativity marks him out as one of the great characters of the New Testament.

FURTHER STUDY

Col. 3:1–10;
2 Cor. 5:17;
Rom. 12:2

1. In what image is the new self made?

2. What are you creating at present?

———— ✦ *Prayer* ✦ ————

O God, help me to turn all common places into creative places. Give me the attitude of Your servant Philip, who turned a routine task into a redemptive one. In Jesus' Name. Amen.

The quiet barrier-smasher

*"The eye is the lamp of the body. If your eyes are
good, your whole body will be full of light."* (v.22)

For reading & meditation – Matthew 6:19–34

e ended yesterday by saying that Philip was one of
the most creative personalities of the New Testament.
He pushed against and broke more barriers than any
other man of his time. Look at some of the barriers he broke:

(1) He was what some would describe today as a "layman" and
he was especially designated to serve at tables. His "job
description" did not include preaching – the task of the apostles.
Listen again to what they had said: "It is not right that we should
give up preaching the word of God to serve tables" (Acts 6:2, RSV).
Yet Philip preached so effectively that he was the only person in
the New Testament designated as "the evangelist" (Acts 21:8).

(2) He was the first missionary – the first to preach the Gospel
beyond Jerusalem. Look at how the Amplified Bible puts the verse
before us today: "Philip (the deacon, not the apostle) went down to
the city of Samaria and proclaimed the Christ, the Messiah, to
them." When the apostles heard of the success of Philip, they sent
down Peter and John to take over the task of introducing them to
the work and ministry of the Holy Spirit.

Does this mean that Philip's ministry comes to an end?
Certainly not. So open is his heart toward God that an angel visits
him and directs him into the desert of Gaza to preach to an
Ethiopian eunuch who, according to tradition, carried the message
of Christ into Africa. Philip's success was not because he rebelled
against the routine into which he was placed, but rather that his
creative spirit lifted him above it. The creative can't help but create.

FURTHER STUDY
Phil. 3:1–14;
Psa. 92:12;
Prov. 4:18

1. What was Paul's
continual attitude?

2. What is the result of
the righteous life?

⊷ *Prayer* ⊶

*O Father, give me, I pray, a creative mind and a creative spirit so that I shall be
able to break through all the barriers that life sets up to hem me in. This I ask
in Jesus' Name. Amen.*

Creativity is contagious

"He had four unmarried daughters who prophesied." (v.9)

For reading & meditation – Acts 21:1–14

We have seen how Philip's creative spirit heightened everything he touched. You can find no evidence of spiritual staleness in Philip's life; he was spiritually alert, spiritually alive and spiritually creative. Our text today tells us that he had four unmarried daughters who prophesied. We must not, of course, ignore the evident work of the Holy Spirit in the lives of these four women, but we must recognize also their father Philip's creative influence in their lives. We often say, "Like father, like son"; here it was a case of "Like father, like daughters." Creativity is contagious.

When you consider that the society in which these daughters were born and brought up was a male-dominated one, the statement that Philip had "four daughters who prophesied" comes as a surprise. What caused these unmarried women to break the mold in which they found themselves and exercise their prophetic gifts? Popular opinion at that time said that women should remain in the background and take no part in public ministry. It was the Holy Spirit, of course, who inspired them to prophesy, but I think I see some of the marks of Philip's creativity rubbing off on them also.

These young women did not stay at home and lament the fact that they were not married. If they could not be creative on a physical level, they could be creative on a spiritual level. Some of the greatest work in the Kingdom of God has been done by the spiritual descendants of the daughters of Philip – single women who have had their creativity blocked on one level, but have released it on another level.

FURTHER STUDY

1 Cor. ch. 7;
Matt. 19:12

1. What does Jesus teach about singleness?

2. How did Paul reinforce this?

⟶ *Prayer* ⟵

Father, I want to thank You today for the ministry of those in Your Kingdom who, while remaining single, have produced great and creative achievements. We appreciate them, but as You have taught us, we give all the honor to You. Amen.

"He died climbing"

"I press on toward the goal to win the prize for which God has called me heavenwards ..." (v.14)

For reading & meditation – Philippians 3:1–14

*W*e spend one more day looking at the importance of being a creative and outgoing person. On the tombstone of an Alpine climber are the words: "He died climbing." That should be on the tombstone of every Christian.

Years ago, at a Christian conference, a missionary who was well into middle age overheard someone say about him: "John has just about shot his bolt." The missionary was so shocked that he left the conference to spend several days in prayer. He came out of the prayer time with a renewed vision, and thirty-five years later was still telling audiences the story of how, in his early fifties, he had found a new lease of life.

A sign frequently seen on British roads is this: "End of reconstruction." While travelling in my car, I saw such a sign and said to a friend who was with me: "Where life is concerned, when you get to the end of reconstruction, you are getting near the end." Life should be a constant process of reconstruction as we allow the Holy Spirit to show us new boundaries to cross, new frontiers to conquer and new challenges to overcome.

A French philosopher has said: "To exist is to change, to change is to mature, to mature is to go on creating oneself endlessly." I would only add one phrase to that: "... to go on creating oneself endlessly – in God." When someone asked a famous architect, then eighty-three, what building he would select as his masterpiece, he replied: "My next one." There is no end to being a Christian, only eternal beginnings. Today can be one of them.

FURTHER STUDY

2 Tim. 4:1–8;
2 Cor. 4:16;
Eph. 4:24

1. What was Paul's testimony?

2. What are we to put on?

⊷⊷ Prayer ⊷⊷

My Lord and my God, help me to push back some frontier today and see some new horizon. Make me sensitive to Your creative impulses that flow through me. And teach me the difference between my impulses and Your own. Amen.

Spiritual digestion

"... his delight is in the law of the Lord, and on his law he meditates day and night." (v.2)

For reading & meditation – Psalm 1:1–6

We come now to what must be considered as one of the highest priorities in our list of suggestions on staying spiritually fresh – cultivate the art of Scripture meditation. For some reason, Bible meditation has become a lost art. A survey conducted among Christians in the United States showed that only one in ten thousand knew how to meditate in the Scriptures.

What, then, is the art of Scripture meditation. Is it reading parts of the Bible as slowly as possible so that every word sinks in? No. Is it studying a passage with the aid of a commentary so that one understands exactly what the Scripture is saying? No. Is it memorizing certain texts and recalling them to mind whenever one has a spare moment? No. You can do all of these things and still not know how to meditate. Andrew Murray describes it as "holding the word of God in your heart and mind until it has affected every area of your life."

My own definition is this: meditation is the process by which we place the Word of God into the digestive system of the soul where it is transformed into faith and spiritual energy. In the psalm before us today there is a picture of amazing freshness and vitality. Listen to it again: "He is like a tree planted by streams of water ... whose leaf does not wither. Whatever he does prospers." What is the secret of this amazing freshness? It is simple – meditation. To draw from Scripture the inspiration and power we need to stay spiritually fresh, we must do more than read it, study it, or even memorize it – we must meditate on it.

FURTHER STUDY

Joshua 1:1–9; 24:31

1. What was God's promise to Joshua?

2. What was the condition – and the result?

⇥ *Prayer* ⇤

O Father, I want so much to learn the art of meditation. Quicken my desire to hide Your word in my heart so that it becomes the hidden springs of action and determines my character and my conduct. In Jesus' Name. Amen.

Why some fear to meditate

"Be still, and know that I am God ..." (v.10)

For reading & meditation – Psalm 46:1–11

DAY
47

*I*n an age of increasing uncertainty, the one sure way of staying on top is by the continuous activity of Scripture meditation. Many Christians, however, are afraid of the word "meditation"; they view it as something practiced by gurus, mystics or the devotees of Eastern religions, and look askance at those who advocate its usefulness and power in the Christian life.

Scripture meditation is as different from that practiced in Eastern religions, however, as chalk is from cheese. They advocate emptying the mind, the Bible advocates filling it – with the truths of God's holy Word. David Ray, an American author and pastor of a large church, says: "I, for one, looked with suspicion on any Christian who advocated the practice of meditation. I thought to myself: 'They are out of touch with reality. Give me action and work, lots of work. Let somebody else waste his time by staring at the end of his nose.' " Then somebody introduced him to the principles of Scripture meditation. He was shown how to place a verse of Scripture on the tip of his spiritual tongue and slowly suck from it the refreshment it contained.

The verse he chose as the focus of his meditation was the one before us today: "Be still, and know that I am God." Take this text now and begin to focus on it. Place it on the tip of your spiritual tongue and draw from it hour by hour the spiritual refreshment that it contains. In your spare moments, pull it to the center of your mind and begin to experience the joy of drawing from God's Word the power He has placed within it.

FURTHER STUDY

1 Pet. 3:1–4;
Job 37:14;
Psa. 131:2;
Isa. 32:17

1. What is of great worth?

2. What advice was given to Job?

⊷ *Prayer* ⊷

Father, I sense that here I am at the crux of this matter of spiritual freshness. Help me not to miss out on any of the lessons You are trying to teach me at this moment in my life. In Jesus' Name. Amen.

The meditation process

"The lazy man does not roast his game ..." (v.27)

For reading & meditation – Proverbs 12:14–28

We continue exploring the meaning of Scripture meditation. One of the synonyms for "meditate" is the word "ruminate." Many animals, such as sheep, goats and cows are ruminant animals. This is because they have stomachs with several compartments – the first of which is called the rumen. The way a ruminant animal digests its food is fascinating. First it literally bolts down its food, and then later regurgitates the food out of its first stomach, the rumen, back into its mouth. This regurgitation process enables the food to be thoroughly digested, whereupon it is absorbed into the animal's bloodstream, so becoming part of its life. Rumination and meditation are parallel words. When a Christian takes a text or phrase from Scripture and turns it over and over in his mind, the truth that is contained in that Scripture is fed into his spiritual digestive system and soon becomes part of his personality. What happened to the breakfast you ate this morning? Assuming you are reading this after breakfast, the meal you have eaten is now being digested and in due course will be distributed to every part of your body in the form of nourishment and energy.

It is the same with meditation. Just as a ruminant animal gets its nourishment and energy from what it eats by regurgitation, so meditation enables a Christian to extract from Scripture the life and energy that is contained within it. So remember, it is not enough just to read the Bible, study the Bible or memorize the Bible. To read the Bible without meditating on it is like chewing one's food without swallowing it.

FURTHER STUDY

Psalm 119:1–176

1. Read this psalm and count the number of times the word "meditation" occurs.

2. What did the psalmist meditate on?

→ *Prayer* ←

Father, the more I see the possibilities within meditation, the more I am on fire to develop it. Help me to maintain this enthusiasm, for I know that Satan will do everything he can to dissuade me. In Jesus' Name. Amen.

"The second thought"

"... let your mind dwell on these things." (v.8, NASB)

For reading & meditation – Philippians 4:4–13

To get the best out of life," said Pascal, "great matters have to be given a *second* thought." Meditation is just that – giving biblical truths a second thought. If you have been thinking that the way to get the best out of the Bible is by reading it, studying it or memorizing it, then I urge you to think again. The way to get the best out of the Bible is by meditating on it.

Reading, studying and memorizing the Bible are, in the main, intellectual exercizes which bring spiritual results. Meditation is not primarily an intellectual exercise but a devotional exercise, a way by which the Word of God is carried into the spiritual digestive system so that it can be translated into spiritual nourishment and energy. Be careful that you do not misunderstand me here. I am not saying that reading, studying and memorizing the Bible are not important spiritual exercizes. I strongly advocate them. But – it is possible to do all these things and yet fail to draw from the Scriptures the spiritual nourishment that God has put within them. That comes largely from meditation.

So that it is crystal clear, let's go over it again: meditation is the process by which we take a text, thought or phrase from the Word of God and roll it around in our mind, passing it backward and forward, letting it go out of conscious thought, bringing it back again into consciousness, prodding it, absorbing it, admiring it over and over again until its inherent power pervades our whole personality. God has gone into His Word and God has to come out of it. Meditation is the way.

FURTHER STUDY

Col. 3:1–16;
Deut. 6:6;
Prov. 4:20–21;
Jer. 15:16

1. What does the word "dwell" mean?

2. How did Jeremiah put it?

⟶ *Prayer* ⟵

O Father, if great matters need a second thought, then help me to slow down and take time to meditate on the truths that are contained in Your precious Word. For Jesus' sake. Amen.

"The unseen Sculptor"

"... as I meditated, the fire burned ..." (v.3)

For reading & meditation – Psalm 39:1–13

Today we ask ourselves: what are the benefits of Scripture meditation? They are beyond telling. Here, however, are just some of the benefits the Bible offers those who will take the time to meditate: (1) success – Joshua 1:8; (2) understanding – Psalm 119:99; (3) an ability to discern between right and wrong – Psalm 119:11. But the one that is most appropriate to our present theme is the one we have already looked at in Psalm 1 – spiritual freshness.

The psalm makes it clear that one of the secrets of staying spiritually fresh is to send one's roots down into the Word of God by meditation. In my teens I knew a man, a miner by trade, whose spiritual freshness and radiance was responsible for turning many people to Jesus Christ. Just before he died, and in the company of several other Christians, I asked him: "What is the secret of your spiritual freshness? You always seem to be on top of things, always radiant ... tell me how you maintain this inner poise and power." He replied in one word – meditation.

I pressed him for some further thoughts on the subject. This is not a verbatim quotation, but as far as I can remember, this is what he said: "Meditation is letting your heart become the workshop of the unseen Sculptor who chisels in its secret chambers the living forms that contribute to character development and an increasing likeness to Jesus Christ." That old man, now in heaven, was one of the greatest illustrations I have ever known of the spiritual freshness and fruitfulness that comes from meditating on God's Word. His experience can be ours – if we meditate.

FURTHER STUDY

Rom. 10:1–9;
Deut. 11:18;
Prov. 6:23;
2 Cor. 3:3

1. What happens when the word is in our hearts?

2. What was Paul's testimony of the Corinthians?

→ Prayer ←

O Father, help me to master the art of meditation, so that through the written Word and by the meditated Word, those around me may see the Living Word. Amen.

A childhood motto

"So if the Son sets you free, you will be free indeed." (v.36)
For reading & meditation – John 8:28–36

We continue looking at ways to stay spiritually fresh. Another suggestion is – examine your life to see that you are not being controlled by hidden agendas. A "hidden agenda," in the sense I am using the phrase, is a negative experience in your past which is influencing your behavior in the present.

Over the years, I have talked to thousands of Christians who have said to me things like this: "I know I am converted and that there is no sin in my life, but yet I seem to be driven by things in my past that I cannot understand. Can you help me?" I have learned to recognize through such conversations that the fears, the hurts and the negative experiences of life can sometimes stay inside us to intrude into our lives, even though we are adults. We think we are being controlled by God but really, deep down, we are being controlled by the experiences of the past that have never really been recognized and dealt with.

During my childhood, I was constantly told: "Big boys don't cry." Thus I came to believe that it was unmanly to cry or show emotion. When I became a Christian, there were times when I felt like crying before the Lord, but would not permit myself to do so. There were times, too, when I felt like crying with a Christian brother or sister who was distressed (see Rom. 12:15, RSV – "weep with those who weep"), but again could not do so. I was controlled by a "hidden agenda," a childhood motto that said, "Big boys don't cry." One day I surrendered the whole situation into God's hands and was free.

FURTHER STUDY
1 Cor. 13:1–11; 14:20;
Gal. 4:3

1. What position did Paul come to?

2. How does this relate to the rest of 1 Corinthians 13?

⊷ *Prayer* ⊷

O Father, I come to You once again to ask for Your help in setting me free from any negative or wrong influences that may be holding me in the past. I want to move forward – not backward. Save me, dear Father. Amen.

52

"Measure up ..."

"Therefore you are no longer a slave, but a son ..." (v.7, NASB)
For reading & meditation – Galatians 4:1–7

What "hidden agendas" are in control of your life? Can you recognize things which are going on inside you which hinder you from experiencing spiritual freshness? Many of you will be aware that there are unhealthy emotional pushes within you that sometimes take you in the direction you do not want to go. You are not the driver – you are being driven.

A minister says that, for forty-nine years, a little childhood motto instilled into him by his parents had been running his life. He says: "For many years I struggled in my Christian life. I was an up-and-down Christian. Outwardly I was successful, but inwardly I was like a yo-yo, bouncing between spiritual highs and lows. Then a flash of insight came to me from the Holy Spirit. I suddenly realized that my life was not really being ruled by love for God, but that a childhood motto which had been drummed into me in my early years had taken over and was controlling me. That childhood motto was this: 'Measure up. The better you do, the more we will love you.'"

The Holy Spirit helped this minister see his "hidden agenda." He came to realize that those two words, "Measure up," carried over from his childhood, were affecting him in his present relationships, including his relationship with God. He was striving to get God to love him when the truth was that God already loved him – not so much for what he did (that was part of it) but for who he was. Instead of living by the wonderful news of the Gospel, he was living by an unseen agenda – in his case, a childhood motto.

FURTHER STUDY

Gal. ch. 5;
John 8:32;
Rom. 8:2

1. What sets us free?

2. What "motto from the past" was affecting some of the Galatian Christians?

↦ *Prayer* ↤

Father, I see how easy it is to be held back from entering into the fullness of Your salvation through some "hidden agenda" that was laid down in my past. Help me now to deal with any such influences in my own life. In Jesus' Name. Amen.

Driven or led – which?

*"Because those who are led by the Spirit of God
are sons of God." (v.14)*

For reading & meditation – Romans 8:1–17

One of the saddest things I have encountered over the years in which I have been attempting to help Christians overcome their problems is to see how many believers are spiritually tied up because of trying to work through a "hidden agenda." Instead of living by the wonderful truths of the Gospel, they are controlled by the directives of some childhood experience. Some of them are experts at expounding Scripture, but their lives are dictated by some inner script which interferes with their spiritual growth and prevents them from staying spiritually fresh. They confess Christ, but are really ruled by a fear, a negative expectation, a hurt, or a wrong assumption from the past.

Does a "hidden agenda" rule your life? Our text today tells us that the true sons and daughters of God are led and controlled by the Holy Spirit. Does the Holy Spirit lead you, or are you driven by some push from the past? Look again at the childhood motto of the minister we looked at yesterday: "Measure up." The implied message in those words was this – "The better you do, the more you will be loved." For many years he thought his life was controlled by Jesus Christ, but the truth was that a childhood motto had become his god and ruled him like a ruthless dictator. He was serving God out of fear rather than love; working to be saved rather than working because he was saved. This is not to say, of course, that God does not want us to "measure up," because He does (Rom. 8:28–29). We must see, however, that His love is not conditional on that.

FURTHER STUDY

John 10:1–11;
Gal. 5:18;
1 Pet. 2:21

1. What is the characteristic of the true shepherd?

2. What is the characteristic of sheep?

⤙ *Prayer* ⤚

O Father, let the wonder of this glorious truth flow deep into my spirit today. Wrap me around in the conviction that I am loved for who I am, not for what I do. I ask this in and through Your peerless and precious Name. Amen.

The enemy within

*"For we know that our old self was crucified with him so that the
body of sin might be done away with ..." (v.6)*

For reading & meditation – Romans 6:1–14

We continue meditating on the issue of "hidden agendas." One question that often comes up is this: "How is it possible for a truly born-again person to have a 'hidden agenda'? Surely such things are cleansed and cleared away when Christ enters a person's heart."

Paul Tournier, in *The Person Reborn,* explains this point in a beautiful way. He says that the Christian experience is like a revolution where a new prince has taken over a country by means of a coup d'etat. Among the crowd that acclaim him are the followers of the fallen king who has now been dethroned. For a little while they seem to be the most enthusiastic supporters of the new regime, but their change of heart is not sincere; they are still loyal to the king and secretly plan to undermine the prince's power.

Tournier says this is similar to what happens at conversion – the elements that went into our early development hide themselves at our conversion and share in the victory we feel. But they have not capitulated and they may later succeed in sabotaging that victory if we do not unmask them. However, the process of unmasking them sometimes takes time and may even require the help of a minister or counselor. Even now, after forty years as a Christian, I sometimes come across a "hidden agenda" in my own life that needs unmasking. When I do, I deal with it right away by surrendering it to the Lord and asking Him to render it inoperative in my life. And does He answer such a prayer? I and thousands of others can testify – He does!

FURTHER STUDY

Rom. 8:12–28;
Psa. 139:23–24;
Col. 2:20;
1 Pet. 2:24

1. What are we to do with the help of the Holy Spirit?

2. Echo the psalmist's prayer today.

⊷ *Prayer* ⊶

My Father and my God, I need Your help to identify any "hidden agendas" that may be operative within me. Show me what they are and help me to lay them at Your feet. In Jesus' Name I ask it. Amen.

Katargeo

*"When I was child ... I thought as a child; but when I
became a man, I put away childish things." (v.11, NKJV)*

For reading & meditation – 1 Corinthians 13:1–13

We spend one last day on the subject of "hidden
agendas." Today we ask ourselves: how do we deal
with these pushes from our past which tend to
influence and control our present attitudes and reactions?

We must fomd how and where they began. They come
especially from the early formative years of childhood. There we
were subjected to influences, ideas and experiences that helped to
shape our expectations and attitudes to life. Many of these
influences, ideas and experiences were good – and this point must
not be overlooked – but by the same token, many were bad. The
negative things sometimes stay inside us and can become
dictating forces in our lives. It needs the help of the Holy Spirit to
track down some of these hidden agendas and we then need to
deal with them in a mature and adult manner.

How do we do this? Look once again at the verse before us
today: "but when I became a man, I put away childish things." The
Greek word for "put away" is *katargeo*. It is an extremely strong
word meaning "to put away, to break a hold, finish it off, have done
with, render inoperative." Childhood agendas don't just fall away
like the leaves fall off the trees in the autumn; we have to "put
them away" – *katargeo* them and be finished with childish things.
If the Holy Spirit has identified any hidden agendas in your life,
then bring them to Him now and lay them at His feet. Decide to
have done with them. Get out of the passenger seat and into the
driving seat. Remember – with God, all things are possible.

FURTHER STUDY

Heb. 12:1–13;
Isa. 55:7;
Eph. 4:22

1. What are we to throw
off?

2. What does "forsake"
mean?

⊷ Prayer ⊷
---

*O Father, give me the victory over all the enemies that may be within me.
Katargeo them – render them inoperative – once and for all. In Jesus' Name.
Amen.*

Gaze on the face of Christ

"But we all ... beholding ... the glory of the Lord, are being transformed into the same image ..." (v.18, NASB)

For reading & meditation – 2 Corinthians 3:7–18

W e come now to our final suggestion for staying spiritually fresh – keep your eyes fully focused on Jesus. Our Lord was the most alert and alive person the world has ever seen. Never once do we read that He experienced spiritual staleness or had to confess to being out of touch with heaven. He was always confident, always assured, always in the right place, doing the right thing at the right time. Even after a period of prolonged fasting in the wilderness when He faced the fiercest of temptations, He returned, not exhausted and limp as a wet rag, but "in the power of the Spirit." Here was spiritual freshness to the *n*th degree.

Our text today tells us that one of the ways by which we can become more and more like Christ is to stand with unveiled faces and continually gaze upon Him. It is a breathtaking concept – and so simple. Yet how profound. Look beyond yourself to Another, and thus free yourself from self-preoccupation. Have you noticed how many of the religious cults get their followers to concentrate on the divinity within them? Then what happens? They finish up preoccupied with their own states of mind and emotion. As someone put it: "If I worship the divinity within me, I will probably end up worshiping myself."

The verse before us today gets our gaze in the right place – on the face of Christ. The attention we give to this is important, for whatever gets our attention gets us. Christ gets our attention, so He gets us. Our gaze must be person-centerd, not problem-centerd. And that Person must be Christ.

FURTHER STUDY

Rom. 8:29–39;
John 1:36;
Col. 2:2–3

1. What is God's plan for us?

2. What was John's declaration?

✦ *Prayer* ✦

Blessed Lord Jesus, when I look at myself I feel unworthy and inadequate. But when I look at You, I feel anything is possible. Help me not just to glance at You, but gaze at You – continuously. Amen.

The "redeemed look"

"Those who look to him are radiant ..." (v.5)
For reading & meditation – Psalm 34:1–22

We saw yesterday the importance of getting our attention focused in the right place. At times it is right to look within ourselves, but we should not spend too much time doing that. Someone put it like this: "If you look long at yourself, you will become discouraged. If you look long at others, you will be distracted. But if you look long at Christ, you will take on His likeness."

You become like that which you gaze at habitually. I meet many people whose faces look like what they are looking at – nothing. No character shows on their face – just a blur. It reminds me of a prospective customer who walked into a shop and enquired: "Do you keep stationery here?" "No." replied the assistant, "we keep moving." Many in this modern age keep moving not only their body but their focus of attention, and the result is a blurred face.

Then I meet others whose faces show they are seeing a Face – the face of Jesus. And their faces are not a blur, but a blessing. A beggar once cried out to a Christian: "You with heaven in your face, please give me a penny." Nietzsche, the famous philosopher, said: "If the Christians want us to believe in Christianity, they must look redeemed." Far too few of us have the redeemed look. The ones that do are those whose gaze is centerd on Jesus. A husband and wife who are deeply in love with one another grow to look like each other. They have looked into the limpid depths of each other's souls for so long that they become like each other in countenance.

FURTHER STUDY
Acts 3:1–16;
John 16:24;
1 Pet. 1:8

1. What was Peter's message?

2. What should be reflected in our faces?

⟶ *Prayer* ⟵

Lord Jesus, You have my heart – have my face too. Let it look as though it belongs to You. Let the light of Your countenance lighten my countenance. In Your Name. Amen.

"I just want to look at you"

"... they saw no one but Jesus only." (v.8, RSV)

For reading & meditation – Matthew 17:1–13

When we gaze at the face of Christ and make Him the center of our attention and love, then we are gradually and continuously changed into the likeness of Christ. Thus we are transformed from one degree of glory to another, the Spirit within us being the silent Artist who makes us into His image. We become like Him in character and in countenance.

A young man was so much like his father in appearance that it prompted everyone who knew him to comment on the fact. The mother said: "It's strange because when Andrew was a small child, he looked so much like me. Then, when he was about five, he became intrigued with being with his father. He used to go into his father's study and sit there until his father would say, 'Is there anything you want?' Andrew would reply, 'No, I don't want anything; I just want to look at you.' He would sit there and lovingly gaze into his father's face for such a long time that I honestly believe this is how he has come to look so much like him."

Just as there is a law in photography that says: "The angle of incidence equals the angle of reflection" – in other words, if you want a full face reproduction, you must look full face into the camera – so there is a law in life that causes us to become like that on which we gaze. If we look sideways on Christ, we get only a partial reflection. If we look fully at Him, we get a full reflection. We become like that on which we gaze.

FURTHER STUDY

Mark 5:1–20;
Luke 23:44–49;
Matt. 27:55–56

1. What was the centurion's response?
2. What did the demoniac do when he saw Jesus?

⊷ *Prayer* ⊷

My Lord and my God, forgive me that so often I just give You a sideways glance when I ought to be continuously gazing into Your Face. Help me to behold You, so that I am transformed from what I am into what You are. Amen.

"The Glory"

*"... as you believe in our Lord Jesus Christ,
who is the Glory ..." (v.1, Moffatt)*

For reading & meditation – James 2:1–13

Can you think of anything that could occupy our attention more profitably than considering how to become more like Jesus? The central condition is the "unveiled face": "And all of us, as with unveiled face, because we continued to behold as in a mirror the glory of the Lord, are constantly being transfigured into His very own image in ever increasing splendor and from one degree of glory to another" (2 Cor. 3:18, Amplified Bible).

Notice, however, that we have to lift the veils if we are to be transformed. When Jesus was crucified, the veil of the temple was rent in two, symbolising the fact that the heart of the universe was laid bare as redemptive love. Since God has unveiled Himself in Jesus, so we in response ought to unveil our faces, drop our masks, gaze in wonder – and in the gazing, be made like Him. It may be that there will be many veils that you will have to lift – veils of dishonesty, hypocrisy, legalism, pride – but I assure you that when they go – He comes.

Just think of it – we who are born of the dust are being gradually transformed into the most beautiful image that this planet has ever seen – the image of Christ. What a destiny. The wonder of that transformation can only be explained by one word – "glory." The drabness, the staleness, the dullness of living is replaced by living that has freshness in it. Can we live continuously like that? Yes – in His strength. "Grace" and "glory" are often connected in the New Testament – take the grace and you get the glory. What a way to live. Glory! Glory! Glory!

FURTHER STUDY

John 1:10–14;
Col. 1:6;
2 Pet. 3:18

1. What were the characteristics of Christ's glory?

2. Make them characteristics of your life this year

↔ *Prayer* ↔

Father, help me to lift every veil in my life so that the light of Your countenance may shine through. You are Light and You want to make me light. Let Your radiance steal into every darkened corner of my being now and forever. Amen.

SECTION TWO

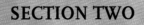

Rebuilding
Broken Walls

Rebuilding Broken Walls

---

*W*alls create a visual image of power. They appear strong, solid, and impenetrable. They present an image of stability and protection. But their defensive value can easily be overestimated, whether they're made of stone and mortar, or of spiritual building blocks like faith, love, and forgiveness. God's message to us is that no wall built for His glory is beyond restoration. Broken walls spur us to act; they are a way for God to direct us in how and where to serve Him.

This series of devotional messages focuses on the story of Nehemiah. However effectively you may be serving the Lord now, the study of Nehemiah will help you serve Him better. Nehemiah left a position of power and influence to return to his people and rebuild the walls of Jerusalem. It was a remarkable testament to his faith that he would make such a sacrifice in the face of such imposing odds.

Thomas Kinkade has put walls in a great many of his paintings. There is an order to them and a sense of security that gives the composition a snug, welcoming feel. It's interesting to notice, though, that every wall is made up of many, many stones or bricks. As he outlines and highlights every one, he sometimes imagines what a difficult job it is to build a real wall, and how devoted to their work the masons must be as they select and fit row after row, day after day. One moment of carelessness or inattention, and the wall could be crooked, its security forever compromised. But diligence and dedication produce a strong, secure – and beautiful – result. Nehemiah never faltered in his faith or his enthusiasm. His story is a wonderfully clear image of God's work being accomplished through the hands of His people. Through rebuilding broken walls of our own, we experience a return to order, completeness, and assurance of our faith. We feel God working through us in a very real and literal way, building within our hearts a new awareness of His restoring power.

L.G.G.

Serving the Lord better

"The words of Nehemiah son of Hacaliah: In the month of Kislev ... I was in the citadel of Susa ..." (v.1)

For reading & meditation – Nehemiah 1:1–11

We embark today on a devotional study of the book of Nehemiah. The main events of the book took place in the spring and summer of the year 445 BC. During this period Nehemiah made the journey from Susa, near the Persian Gulf, to the city of Jerusalem in order to restore the city's ruined defenses. His story is regarded by many as one of the liveliest in the Bible. The late Dr. Martyn Lloyd-Jones said: "No one leaps out of the pages of the Old Testament and grabs your attention as does Nehemiah." I agree.

I have invited you on this first day to read the introductory chapter to help you get into the book. However, it is my intention (starting tomorrow) to deal with the whole of Nehemiah's memoirs verse by verse or section by section. My main purpose today is to outline what you can expect to get from this book as we progress through it.

As a young man I was told that whatever career I chose for myself, I would never be able to serve the Lord effectively until I understood the principles set out in the book of Nehemiah. I found that advice to be true. To enter into any career, whether in the business world or the Christian ministry, without an understanding of the spiritual principles that hold life together is utter foolishness. And many of those principles are illustrated most powerfully in the story of Nehemiah. I give you this promise – however effectively you may be serving the Lord now, the study of Nehemiah will help you serve Him better.

FURTHER STUDY

**Gen. 24:34–49;
Dan. 6:6–16**

1. Why did God answer the prayer of Abraham's servant?

2. Why was Daniel calm despite the plot against him?

⊷ *Prayer* ⊷

My Father and my God, help me understand even more deeply than I do at present that only as far as my life is in tune with Your will can it be said to be successful. Teach me more of what I really need to know. In Jesus' Name. Amen.

First things first

*"Hanani, one of my brothers, came from Judah with
some other men, and I questioned them ..." (v.2)*

For reading & meditation – Nehemiah 1:1–2

When we first meet Nehemiah, he is serving as cupbearer (winetaster) in Susa, the principal palace and winter residence of the Persian kings. Nehemiah was a Jew, of course, probably of the tribe of Judah, but as cupbearer to the king he held a position of great eminence. As Nehemiah begins his story he tells of receiving a visit from his brother, Hanani, who reports that the gates and walls of Jerusalem are broken down. The Temple, rebuilt under Haggai and Zechariah, was still intact, but because of the decline in spirituality and general apathy, the city walls had been allowed to lie in ruins. In addition to this, marauders had burned down the gates and reduced them to a pile of ashes. Jerusalem, the city of God, was in a sorry state. Nehemiah's strong reaction to this news shows us where his real concerns lay: not in maintaining a good position in the Persian Empire but in achieving God's purposes for His holy city.

What, I wonder, is our reaction when we observe some of the modern "walls" which God has inspired and instructed His people to build now in a state of disrepair? Take, for example, the issue of marriage and family life. The walls that buttressed this most precious institution are in danger of being demolished. "Marriages are a thing of the past," says an article in one journal. "Wedding rings are doomed." How do we react when we see God's principles disregarded, His "walls" being broken down? Do our personal concerns take priority over God's concerns? Nehemiah put first things first. So must we.

FURTHER STUDY

Matt. 5:27–32;
1 Cor. 5:1–13;
Rev. 21:10–27

1. If churches rebuilt walls by fully obeying Scripture, would the neediest be excluded?

2. How does John see the problem resolved?

✦ *Prayer* ✦

O God, forgive us if we have been putting our personal ambitions before Your concerns and the affairs of Your kingdom. Give us the same spirit that Nehemiah had, who made Your priorities his priorities. In Christ's Name we pray. Amen.

Face it and feel it

"... 'Those who survived the exile and are back in the province are in great trouble and disgrace.' " (v.3)

For reading & meditation – Nehemiah 1:3

We look now in more detail at the way in which Nehemiah reacted when he heard that the walls of Jerusalem were still in ruins and that the city gates had been burned to the ground. "I sat down and wept," he admits (v.4). I know some Christians who, had they been with Nehemiah at that moment, would have slapped him on the back and said: "Stop crying, Nehemiah. God is on the throne, and He'll bring His purposes to pass no matter how bad things appear to be." It is, of course, entirely true that God is on the throne and brings good out of bad, but that truth ought not to be used to deny or repress the legitimate feelings of sorrow. The first thing to do when confronted by a disaster or loss is to face it and feel it.

A number of Christians think that because we are "partakers of the divine nature" we should never feel sad. And if we do, then we should pretend that we don't. This attitude has led a group of non-Christian psychologists in the United States to invent a new psychological condition for Christians who deny their true feelings: "eclessiogenic neurosis."

Regardless of our spiritual maturity, we will feel the pain of misfortune or loss acutely. To pretend that we do not is evidence of immaturity. We are not to wallow in these emotions but we must be willing to feel them, for unacknowledged emotions cause trouble. Integrity requires that whatever is true must be faced – and that includes troublesome emotions. Nehemiah was no less godly because he gave vent to his emotions. It's the healthy thing to do.

FURTHER STUDY

Heb. 10:32–39;
1 Pet. 3:15–17; 4:12–19

1. What were those who had experienced hardship to hold on to?

2. What does Peter say our response to trouble should be?

⇥ *Prayer* ⇤

O Father, help me see that facing and feeling the emotions that arise within me is not a sign of faithlessness. I don't have to stay there but I do have to start there. Rid me of all confusion on this matter. In our Lord's Name I pray. Amen.

Weeping over the ruins

"The wall of Jerusalem is broken down, and its gates have been burned with fire." (v.3)

For reading & meditation – Nehemiah 1:3

As we consider how Nehemiah wept over Jerusalem, it seems appropriate to remember that he wasn't the only person to weep over the holy city. Our Lord wept for Jerusalem too. Letting things affect us emotionally is not a sign of lack of faith in God, but we must not allow those matters to drag us down into self-pity. God's strength and resources are given to us not so that we can deny our feelings but to support us in them and bring us through.

Nehemiah's intensely emotional reaction to the news concerning the plight of Jerusalem highlights the first of the many spiritual principles we shall discover in following his story: before anyone can receive a blessing, someone else has to be willing to bear a burden. We can never lighten the load for others until we have first felt the weight of their troubles in our own soul. Nehemiah was not ready to put into action any kind of recovery plan for Jerusalem until he had first faced his feelings and wept because of its ruined state. Likewise, we are fit to do God's work only when we have faced matters and recognized how they are in reality – accepted the truth about a situation.

Look around you today and see things as they are, not as you would like them to be. Are you aware of any broken-down "walls"? The walls of your devotional life perhaps. Your family. Your church. Is there something for which you should be grieving at this moment? A ruin you are not prepared to acknowledge? Remember, you can't begin to rebuild a crumbling wall unless first you are willing to mourn over it.

FURTHER STUDY

Ex. 3:7–12; 4:10–16;
Jer. 1:4–9

1. Why did Moses and Jeremiah object when called by God?

2. What was the common element in their enabling?

━━◈ *Prayer* ◈━━

O God, help me to see things as they are, not as I would like them to be. Help me discover if there are any ruins in my life and, if so, recognize them and grieve over them. In Jesus' Name. Amen.

Attitude fixes altitude

*"For some days I mourned and fasted and prayed
before the God of heaven." (v.4)*

For reading & meditation – Nehemiah 1:4–7

We are discovering that there can be no spiritual progress until we have looked intently at things and perceived them as they really are. Walls cannot be rebuilt until we see – and see clearly – the ruins in which they lie. When we have a vision of spiritual ruin we are tempted to exclaim: "We are helpless to do anything about it." But what should we do after such moments of revelation? We should do what Nehemiah did – turn to fervent, believing prayer.

Look with me now at Nehemiah's prayer. Clearly, he was a man whose soul had been fed on the Word of God. His words were cast in the mold of God's revelation of Himself as given in the Scriptures – a characteristic of all great prayer warriors. He reminds the Almighty of His greatness and His awesomeness and the fact that He is a covenant-keeping God. He stands in both awe and adoration before Him, recognizing His sovereignty. The greater God becomes to him, the smaller his problem appears in comparison. Nehemiah is then moved to confess the sins of his people and admits that their troubles stemmed from disobedience. Usually sin is the cause of our failures, and where there is sin it must always be confessed.

The attitude underlying Nehemiah's prayer is important to note: it is an attitude of reverence and submission. One person has said: "The self-sufficient do not pray; they merely talk to themselves. The self-satisfied will not pray; they have no knowledge of their need. The self-righteous cannot pray; they have no basis on which to come to God." When there is no reverence for God, there will be few answers from God.

FURTHER STUDY

Joel 2:12–13;
2 Chron. 7:14;
Psa. 66:18

1. What type of mourning is acceptable to God?

2. When does the Lord hear prayer?

→ Prayer ←

Father, help me learn that in this matter of prayer I ascend to the heights not by reason of my words alone, but by the attitude which underlies them. The attitude determines the altitude. Teach me to pray, dear Lord, as You once taught Your disciples. Amen.

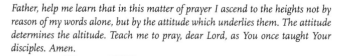

The Promise-Keeper

*"O Lord, let your ear be attentive to the prayer
of this your servant ..." (v.11)*

For reading & meditation – Nehemiah 1:8–11

For another day we reflect on Nehemiah's powerful prayer. In claiming the provision God made for His people, the godly Nehemiah reveals another great principle, namely that prayer must be based on God's promises. "Remember Your instructions to Moses," he says, and then, paraphrasing the words the Lord gave to Moses, he claims the fulfilment of the promise. Nehemiah's confidence in the Lord as a promise-keeper is so great that he knows God will work out the details. Finally the prayer closes with a request that God will give him favor with the king of Persia – King Artaxerxes. Nehemiah knows it will be harder for him to leave the court than it was to enter it. He is a trusted and important man. But he accepts, too, that with God all things are possible.

Many commentators point out that the prayer pattern Nehemiah followed parallels the "outline" of prayer which our Lord gave in Luke 11. But prayer depends on more than just keeping to a pattern. It has been said: "God does not hear our prayers so much as hears us" – in other words, what we put of ourselves into our prayers. Nehemiah continued entreating the Lord's favor for four months! [Nov./Dec. (1:1) to Mar./Apr. (2:1)]. "Persistence in prayer," as the old saying goes, "is what makes the difference."

Do we hear Nehemiah's kind of praying nowadays? Sadly, not as often as we ought. Most modern-day prayers are token prayers asking God to bless this, that and the other. Powerful praying flows out of seeing the situation as it is. And in seeing God as He is.

FURTHER STUDY

Luke 18:1–8;
Matt. 6:7–8;
Eccl. 5:2

1. How can the different instructions on prayer be reconciled?

2. When is repetition ineffective?

⊷ *Prayer* ⊷

My Father and my God, enable me to see things as they really are and to see You as You really are. Then help me to fuse You and the need together in fervent believing prayer. Amen.

The waiting test

*"... the king asked me, 'Why does your face look
so sad when you are not ill?'" (v.2)*

For reading & meditation – Nehemiah 2:1–2

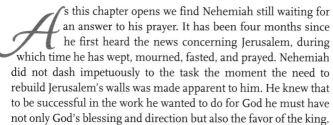

s this chapter opens we find Nehemiah still waiting for
an answer to his prayer. It has been four months since
he first heard the news concerning Jerusalem, during
which time he has wept, mourned, fasted, and prayed. Nehemiah
did not dash impetuously to the task the moment the need to
rebuild Jerusalem's walls was made apparent to him. He knew that
to be successful in the work he wanted to do for God he must have
not only God's blessing and direction but also the favor of the king.

During a royal banquet Nehemiah gives wine to the king, and
something in Nehemiah's facial expression causes the king to
express his concern. Artaxerxes invites Nehemiah to share with
him the reason for his sadness, which of course he does. The
burden of his heart, the deep conviction of his soul, need no longer
be hidden. The initiative is no longer in Nehemiah's hands; it is in
God's.

How important is timing in all that we seek to do for God. Many
a life has been shipwrecked spiritually because of impulsiveness
and haste. I know people who could have been in a great ministry
today but they failed the waiting test. They sensed a need, and did
not wait for God's perfect timing in the matter. There are those
who say the need is the call. Though there is some truth in that, it
must be balanced by the fact that God's timing must be sought in
everything we do. A right action can turn out to be wrong simply
because it was mistimed. God's timing is always perfect. Ours is
not.

FURTHER STUDY

Gen. 12:4; 25:7;
Ex. 7:7;
Deut. 34:7;
Luke 3:23

1. What do 75/175,
80/120, 30/33 reveal
about God's training
schedules?

2. Are you willing to
wait for His perfect

⊷ *Prayer* ⊷

*O Father, show me even more clearly the need to adjust my spiritual clock to
Yours. Help me be alert not only to what You are calling me to do but the right
time in which I should set out to do it. In Jesus' Name. Amen.*

Prayer-o-grams

"Then I prayed to the God of heaven ..." (v.4)

For reading & meditation – Nehemiah 2:3–5

*I*n response to the king's question concerning his sad countenance, Nehemiah loses no time in requesting permission to visit Jerusalem in order to help his people restore the city to its former glory. Before making his petition to the king, we see him sending off a prayer-o-gram to the Almighty. Even though the initiative has come from the king, Nehemiah senses his need of divine help as he makes his petition known.

How different things might be if we could learn to lift our hearts in prayer whenever we face a difficult or delicate situation. I don't mean "token praying" – praying for the sake of it. The kind of prayer I am talking about here is not so much bending the knee in supplication or even a particular form of words but the attitude of spirit that says: "Lord, help me draw on Your resources as I face this difficult moment." Having said this, it is important that Nehemiah's detailed request was not something that resulted from his prayer-o-gram. That was a quick request for help as he presented his petition, but you can be sure that the details of that petition had been worked out in hours of prolonged intercession over a period of four months. How persistently Nehemiah must have sought the Lord, and how passionately he must have pleaded with God concerning his position at the court.

Prayer-o-grams have their place, but they must never be seen as substitutes for fervent, believing intercession. We would all like to be able to pray Ford prayers and get Rolls-Royce blessings. But some rewards in prayer come only in proportion to the effort.

FURTHER STUDY

Gen. 32:22–30;
Luke 6:12

1. Reflect today on the strength of Jacob's and Jesus' praying.

2. Wrestling or nestling? Is there a place for both in one's prayer life?

⊶ *Prayer* ⊶

Father, I see there is a place for prayer-o-grams and a place for persistent intercession. Help me understand the purpose of both and utilize both. In Jesus' Name I pray. Amen.

Safe, sent and supplied

*"And because the gracious hand of my God was
upon me, the king granted my requests." (v.8)*

For reading & meditation – Nehemiah 2:6–9

*J*ust how profitable the four months were that Nehemiah
spent fasting and praying can be seen from the well
thought-out presentation he made to the king. Clearly
divine wisdom had been at work, enabling him to put together
a petition that covered his every need.

Only one person had the resources to help rebuild the city of
Jerusalem – Artaxerxes. As he prayed, Nehemiah would have
become aware of what was required to successfully complete the
assignment, such as a safe passage through the different
provinces, which only the king's seal would guarantee. This point,
therefore, is included in his request. One of the king's forests was
close to Jerusalem, and thus he asks the king for a letter of
authority to present to the man in charge. Was he asking for too
much? Certainly not! The king was well able to give him all he
asked, and these things were essential if the task, once begun, was
to be completed.

This ought to encourage us to be bold in our praying. As the
hymnist put it: "We are coming to a King. Large petitions we must
bring." Though Nehemiah had worked hard on his petition, he
does not take the credit when the king grants his requests. Rather,
he sees it as evidence of the gracious hand of the Lord upon him
(v.8). Nehemiah must have been greatly heartened before setting
out on his journey to know he had been sent by the king, had his
guarantee of a safe passage, and that all his needs would be
supplied. Sent, safe, supplied – all these things are supremely
important if we are to be successful in what we do for God.

FURTHER STUDY

Gen. 45:1–15;
1 Kings 17:1–16;
Matt. 2:13–23

1. Joseph, Elijah and
Joseph – what 2 factors
are common to their
experience?

2. When did they realize
they were safe, sent and
supplied?

✦ *Prayer* ✦

---

*O Father, help me to have Nehemiah's dependent and humble attitude and never
to boast about the things that You accomplish through me as if I had done them
unaided. This I ask in our Lord's precious and peerless Name. Amen.*

Are we known in hell?

*"When Sanballat ... and Tobiah ... heard about this,
they were very much disturbed ..." (v.10)*

For reading & meditation – Nehemiah 2:10

In this verse we are told that when Sanballat, the governor of Samaria, and Tobiah his associate knew that Nehemiah was on his way to Jerusalem they were extremely displeased. These two men throw a long dark shadow over the story. They were men of influence and power who opposed and tried to outmaneuver Nehemiah in everything that he did. Sanballat and Tobiah knew perfectly well what Nehemiah was after – the restoration of the holy city. Being enemies of God they would focus their hatred not only on the Lord but on His servant also.

One thing becomes apparent from a study of Christian history and it is this: whenever anyone says, "Let us arise and build," Satan and his forces respond: "Let us arise and stop him." About 50,000 Jews were living in Judah but there appeared to be little concern among them about the state of Jerusalem's walls and the ruined testimony of their Jewish faith. Once it was known, however, that Nehemiah was on his way to rebuild Jerusalem, war was declared in the heavens. No battle can commence anywhere, in the spiritual sense, until somebody decides to stand up and challenge the things that need challenging.

How much overtime has the devil to put in, I wonder, because of our willingness to stand up and do something for God? Or to put it another way: How well are we known in hell? One thing is sure – when we stand up and are counted as citizens of the kingdom, then Satan will throw all his weight against us. If you don't want a spiritual battle then stay seated.

FURTHER STUDY

Eph. 6:10–18;
Rev. 12:7–12;
Luke 10:17–20

1. Where must our preparation for spiritual warfare begin?

2. What is the theme of the victory celebrations?

⤳ *Prayer* ⤳

O God, how can I stay seated when so much is at stake? Some of the walls of Your kingdom have been flattened by unbelief and neglect. Give me the same kind of courage that Nehemiah had – the courage to stand up and be counted. In Christ's Name. Amen.

While others slept ...

"I had not told anyone what my God had put in my heart to do for Jerusalem." (v.12)

For reading & meditation – Nehemiah 2:11–16

After a journey of about two months, Nehemiah arrives safely in Jerusalem. Though he is a man of action, he takes time to brief himself on the situation and, after waiting three days, sets out on horseback to survey the city walls. Presumably he toured the city at night so as not to alert Israel's enemies to his intentions too early.

Nehemiah's tour of inspection takes him out through the Valley Gate. In some places the debris is so widespread that he is forced to dismount and make his way over the ruins by foot. Then, after surveying the whole city, he returns through the same gateway. We can only conjecture as to what Nehemiah felt as he reconnoitered. Jerusalem had once been a mighty fortress with its walls standing tall and strong. Now it was in a sad state. How he must have wept as he took in the distressing picture.

Whenever a work is about to be undertaken for God, some faithful burdened soul has to make a similar journey: to identify the difficulties, to weep in the night over the ruins, to wrestle in some dark Gethsemane in prayer. Some Christians believe that we should not even look at anything negative in case it becomes an impediment to faith. What kind of faith is it that can't be upheld while facing things as they really are? We don't have to linger over negative situations, but we do have to look at them. All great movements of God begin with someone who, like Nehemiah, is brave enough to look fully at the facts, analyze what should be done, then rise to the task.

FURTHER STUDY

1 Sam. 3:1–18; 26:7–12

1. What did Samuel receive while Eli slept?
2. What point was David trying to make when Saul was asleep?

⊷ *Prayer* ⊷

My Father and my God, help me understand how to be a realist without being a pessimist. Teach me how to take a short look at problems and a long look at You. I ask it in and through the precious Name of Jesus. Amen.

"Come, let us rebuild"

*"Come, let us rebuild the wall of Jerusalem,
and we will no longer be in disgrace." (v.17)*

For reading & meditation – Nehemiah 2:17–18

At the end of three days and a night, during which time Nehemiah made his inspection of the city walls, there must have been a great deal of interest as to the real purpose of his visit. Being the strategist he was, Nehemiah knew that by keeping the purpose of his visit secret, the people's curiosity would be greatly heightened.

Once he is in possession of the facts, he convenes a meeting of all the inhabitants, and draws their attention to the need for a careful evaluation of their plight. "You see the trouble we are in," he says, "Jerusalem lies in ruins ... Come, let us rebuild the wall ... and we will no longer be in disgrace." This is exactly the kind of talk the people needed.

Sometimes with spiritual matters our view becomes clouded by familiarity and we need someone with a clearer spiritual perspective to confront us and say: "This is not the way things should be." How about you? Look around you right now. Are there "walls" in your life lying flat that should be standing? Perhaps once you were on fire for God but now you rationalize your Christian experience and comment: "Life nowadays is tough. I can't be expected to be on top of things all the time." Dangerous thinking.

Permit me to come alongside you and say: "Take a look around. See the walls that are lying flat? That is not what God wants. Ruined walls do not glorify God. Come, let us rebuild – and without delay."

FURTHER STUDY

Gal. 1:6–9; 3:1–9;
5:7–10;
Heb. 3:12–14; 6:1–2;
10:22–25

1. Do any of the Galatians passages challenge you?

2. If so, be encouraged by the passages from Hebrews.

⟶ *Prayer* ⟵

O Father, Your Word pierces and penetrates and strikes like an arrow deep into my soul. I hear Your call to rebuild – and I respond. I will take the first steps toward this today. Help me dear Father. In Jesus' Name. Amen.

"In Jesus' Name, get out!"

"The God of heaven will give us success." (v.20)

For reading & meditation – Nehemiah 2:19–20

ow true it is (as we said earlier) that when we hear the challenge "Come, let us rebuild" Satan quickly marshals his forces and says: "Come, let us destroy." Sanballat, Tobiah and Geshem the Arab (another powerful ruler) are at hand to oppose Nehemiah. "What is this you are doing?" they ask. "Are you rebelling against the king?" (v.19). An insinuation that the Jews were rebelling against King Artaxerxes had previously been sufficient to cause work in Jerusalem to cease (Ezra 4:11–23). Sanballat, Tobiah and Geshem try the same tactic again, knowing that demoralized people are inclined to give way when threatened. But they reckon without Nehemiah! Before the Jews have time to react, Nehemiah answers the evil triumvirate: "The God of heaven will give us success. We his servants will start rebuilding. But as for you, you have no share in Jerusalem or any claim or historic right to it" (v.20).

How desperately we need men and women in the Church today who will stand up to the devil and say: "Make all the threats you like. We will not be diverted from our purpose of building walls in God's kingdom and bringing praise to our King." Nehemiah's confidence was not in his mandate from King Artaxerxes but in his commission from the King of heaven. This is why he is able to stand up to the enemies of God and say in effect: "I am standing on God's territory – and you have no right to be anywhere near it." Satan is camped on much of God's property nowadays. It's time to say to him: "In Jesus' Name, get out!"

FURTHER STUDY

Luke 11:24–26; 7:18–23

1. What did Jesus teach about Satan and his forces?

2. Draw encouragement from the signs Jesus reported.

✦ *Prayer* ✦

O Father, forgive us for our timidity when facing Satan and his forces. We know we are no match for him in our own name, but in Your Name there is just no contest. Help us rise up and resist him. For Your own dear Name's sake. Amen.

First principles

"Eliashib the high priest and his fellow priests went to work and rebuilt the Sheep Gate." (v.1)

For reading & meditation – Nehemiah 3:1–2

*I*n response to Nehemiah's rousing challenge "Come, let us rebuild" it appears that all the local inhabitants turn up for work. Under his inspiring leadership, the first to get going are the priests. This group might easily have absolved themselves from an obligation to work on the wall by pleading their calling and consecration to sacred things. So it is to their credit that they take the lead in the rebuilding program. And having a service of dedication after their work they sound the right spiritual note for others to follow. You will notice that each paragraph in this chapter deals with one of the gates of Jerusalem, beginning at the Sheep Gate and moving counterclockwise around the city.

It must have been an amazing sight to see Eliashib the High Priest and all the other priests giving themselves enthusiastically to the task of rebuilding the wall. Management experts tell us one of the first principles of leadership is coordination. This involves blending people and their activities together in a way that successfully contributes to the whole. This is a principle we are going to notice much at work in this chapter.

While the Church should not think of itself as a business affair, it ought nevertheless to be businesslike in all its affairs. coordination is needed as greatly in the Church as it is in business. Those churches with the pastor-does-it-all approach will never develop properly. Such an attitude curbs the ministry which God has given to every believer. No coordination – no corporate or individual development and growth. It is as simple as that.

FURTHER STUDY

Matt. 5:23–24;
Mark 3:31–35; 10:17–22;
Luke 9:57–62; 14:25–27

1. What first principles are set out here?

2. Which are as valid for the Church as the individual?

⤐ *Prayer* ⤏ ---

Father, I see there are right ways and wrong ways to do things – whether in the Church or in the world. Raise up many more modern-day Nehemiahs to help coordinate the latent abilities in Your Church. In Jesus' Name. Amen.

What's your gift?

*"Next to him Meshullam ... made repairs,
and next to him Zadok ..." (v.4)*

For reading & meditation – Nehemiah 3:3–4

The phrase in this verse that I want to focus on with you is one that we shall see occurring time and again in this chapter: "next to him" or "next to them." Nehemiah knew where each person or group would work and the kind of work for which they were best suited. What a different climate there would be in the Church if the leaders helped people to discover their basic gifts. Then everyone would do what they are best suited to doing rather than functioning as square pegs in round holes.

Have you discovered yet where you belong in Christ's Body? For many years I have been concerned by the large number of Christians who have no idea of their basic spiritual gift (or gifts). I believe that every Christian has *at least* one basic spiritual gift, and that if that gift is not discovered and developed then the person can soon fall prey to discouragement and disillusionment – perhaps even despair. Some serious heart-searching needs to be done if spiritual growth and development are to be experienced. We don't drift into maturity; we develop through prayer and careful thought.

When you have no understanding of what your basic gift is, then it is likely that you will go through life producing minimum effectiveness with maximim weariness. When you do understand what your basic gift is – I promise you – you will go through life achieving maximum effectiveness with minimum weariness.

FURTHER STUDY

Luke 19:11–26;
Acts 9:36–39;
1 Cor. 12:4–11; 12:27;
14:5; 14:12

1. Who suffers if you do not exercise your spiritual gifts?

2. Which gifts have been entrusted to you?

⊱ *Prayer* ⊰

O Father, am I a square peg in a round hole? Help me to discover my basic spiritual gift so that I can be effective. In Jesus' Name. Amen.

The unbending neck

"... but their nobles would not put their shoulders to the work under their supervisors." (v.5)

For reading & meditation – Nehemiah 3:3–5

ailure to understand one's role in Christ's Body results in one's service for Christ becoming a hit-or-miss affair. You will have noticed, I am sure, that the churches which are forging ahead and reaching out into their communities have leaders who understand this principle and help their people discover and develop their basic spiritual gift.

Look with me now at the passage before us today. First we see the sons of Hassenaah at work rebuilding the Fish Gate. This was one of Jerusalem's key gates, and doubtless the workers gave themselves to the task of reconstruction with energy, enthusiasm and skill. However, there is one jarring note in these verses: "The next section was repaired by the men of Tekoa, but their nobles would not put their shoulders to the work under their supervisors." The prophet Amos, you remember, was from Tekoa; I wonder what he would have said about these aristocrats who disliked the idea of throwing themselves into the work of rebuilding!

FURTHER STUDY

Ex. 32:1–14; 32:30–33;
Matt. 5:3–10

1. What did Moses do to secure forgiveness for his people?

2. What is promised to those who avoid pride?

Their problem, I think, was not so much lethargy as pride. The word translated "shoulders" in the text means "back of the neck" and is taken from the imagery of oxen refusing to yield to the yoke. The unbending neck is a standard picture of pride in the Bible. Pride, we must not forget, was the very first sin. It turned an angel into the devil. There will never be much spiritual progress where there is pride. Keep this always in mind – pride must die in us if Christ is to live in us.

⊹⊸ *Prayer* ⊸⊹

Lord Jesus Christ, help me reflect on the significance of these words – that if pride doesn't die in me, You will not be able to live in me. Deliver me from the unbending neck and an unbiddable attitude. For Your own dear Name's sake. Amen.

T-e-a-m-w-o-r-k

*"... repairs were made by men from Gibeon and Mizpah ...
places under the ... governor of Trans-Euphrates." (v.7)*

For reading & meditation – Nehemiah 3:6–7

We have seen over the past couple of days evidence of Nehemiah's skills as a leader – he put every person in the place where they belonged. This is known, we said, as the principle of coordination. Another important principle of leadership is cooperation. Even the most superficial reading of this third chapter illustrates Nehemiah's ability to get people to work closely together. Under God he brings together a powerful taskforce from different walks of life – priests, Levites, rulers and common people, merchants, Temple servants, guards, farmers, goldsmiths.

I heard one management expert say the word "success" should be spelled "t-e-a-m-w-o-r-k." His observation that "if the whole prospers the individual will prosper" deserves emphasis. Notice how in the reconstruction of the Jeshanah Gate we read that repairs were carried out by men from Gibeon and Mizpah. These had little to gain by fortifying Jerusalem as they lived some distance from the city. They could easily have allowed their own interests to draw them away from such personally unrewarding work. Yet God's purpose for Jerusalem was that its walls should be a symbol of salvation and its gates a symbol of praise. We can safely assume, I think, that though they did'nt live near Jerusalem it was a matter of great concern to them that these symbols of God's glory should be restored.

The point has been made before – if we belong to Christ then all personal preoccupations and interests ought to be secondary to the building up of His kingdom. Nothing, nothing must take precedence over this.

FURTHER STUDY

Josh. 6:1–5; 6:15–16; 6:20;

Luke 10:1–3; 10:17–20

1. What relevance does the story of Jericho have today?

2. What can we learn from Luke about teamwork?

⋆⇢ *Prayer* ⇠⋆

Father, I take this challenge to heart once again. Help me evaluate my time and activities in the light of Your kingdom. Give me grace to make Your priorities my priorities. In Christ's Name I pray. Amen.

Side by side

"Shallum ... repaired the next section with the
help of his daughters." (v.12)

For reading & meditation – Nehemiah 3:8–12

Although the word cooperation is not mentioned anywhere in the chapter now under consideration, it is clear that Nehemiah was skilful in getting men and women from all walks of life to cooperate in the rebuilding of Jerusalem's walls. The priests (as we said) could easily have excused themselves from the work by reason of the fact that they were called to more spiritual activities. The goldsmiths could have excused themselves on the grounds that their hands were not used to such rough work. The rulers could have insisted on being supervisors, but instead they labored shoulder to shoulder with the others.

In one of the verses before us today we see a goldsmith and a perfume-maker working side by side to rebuild the Jeshanah Gate – more evidence of Nehemiah's ability to get people to cooperate. We see also that one of the officials, a man named Shallum, was being assisted by his daughters. These young women showed they were not afraid to soil their hands with work normally done by men. How was Nehemiah able to get people from different walks of life to cooperate with each other in this way? It was by his inspiring leadership and example. The godly Nehemiah was able to set before them the vision of what ought to be done, then fire them with the importance of that task.

How desperately we stand in need of such leadership in the Church today. Is not the whole issue of strong and godly leadership one to which our praying ought to be directed?

FURTHER STUDY

Judg. 6:11–16; 7:2–7;
7:16–21;
Luke 5:1–11

1. What qualities do leaders need?

2. What are the demands and results of working side by side?

—————— ✦ *Prayer* ✦ ——————

Father, help me to be part of the movement of the Spirit that prays for the kind of leadership that both the Church and the world stand in need of. Perhaps it is true we get the leaders we deserve. Help us. In Jesus' Name. Amen.

Expressing appreciation

"They also repaired five hundred yards of the wall as far as the Dung Gate." (v.13)

For reading & meditation – Nehemiah 3:13–14

We look now at what management experts consider is a third principle of successful leadership – commendation. By this is meant a readiness to note and praise honest effort and to take a personal interest in those for whom one is responsible. Although in this third chapter we do not see Nehemiah actively going around praising people, we certainly see him taking a strong personal interest in his workers.

Some might find the recital of the names of all the people who worked on the different gates somewhat tedious, but it reveals a lot about Nehemiah's awareness of who each person was, what they did and where they worked. It comes across also in the oft-repeated word "repairs." The repetition of this word shows us how ready Nehemiah was to observe and appreciate the work that was being done. This is seen even more clearly, I think, in the verse in which we are told that Hanun and the residents of Zanoah repaired five hundred yards of broken-down wall (v.13), while next to them, Malkijah, working alone, repaired only the Dung Gate (v.14). Nehemiah, however, included both in the list of people commended, and did not allow the extent of one person's accomplishments to prevent him from recognizing the efforts of another. In Nehemiah's eyes every person was valued and was not to be manipulated or exploited.

Every one of us needs to feel that we count for something. I know I do, and I am sure you do also. God, of course, appreciates us. Scripture leaves us in no doubt about that. But it's nice to be appreciated by other human beings also.

FURTHER STUDY

Gen. 41:1–16; 41:28–45;
Matt. 25:14–23;
Luke 17:11–19

1. When we receive praise, why must we give God the glory?

2. Recall the past week – have you thanked God for everything?

↦ *Prayer* ↤

O God, forgive me if, when I feel unappreciated, I use that fact as an excuse for not expressing appreciation to others. This is not how You want me to live. Make me more interested in giving than getting. In Jesus' Name. Amen.

"Good work, Malkijah"

"The Dung Gate was repaired by Malkijah ... ruler of the district of Beth Hakkerem." (v.14)

For reading & meditation – Nehemiah 3:14–27

W̲e continue thinking about the third principle of successful leadership – commendation. As with the words coordination and cooperation, this term is not actually mentioned, but the principle can be discovered nevertheless. The point that leaps out from almost every verse in this chapter is that Nehemiah was aware of the position of each of his workers and knew them all by name.

Today we live in an age of depersonalization. Far too often we are identified on computer files by numbers rather than names. Some of the retailers from whom we purchase goods (not all) are more concerned about our credit rating than they are with the quality of the products they sell to us. I read recently about some psychologists who conducted an experiment on a group of volunteers who were isolated for a month and referred to by number rather than by name. At the end of the month's experiment each member of the group experienced depression to a varying degree, and all appeared to suffer from a temporary loss of self-worth. I am so glad that in eternity we are not going to get a number but a new name (Rev. 2:17).

It is my belief that a man who demonstrated so much care in recording the names of all who worked on the rebuilding of the wall must have shown that same kind of concern in his personal relationships with them day by day. "Good work, Malkijah," I can hear him say. "And you too, Hananiah." Mark Twain commented that he could live for a whole month on a compliment. It's sad that we are far more ready to criticize than commend.

FURTHER STUDY

John 1:1–2;
1 John 1:1–3;
Phil. 2:5–11;
Rev. 19:11–16

1. What does the description of Jesus as "the Word" tell us?

2. Why did God give Him that Name?

⤐ *Prayer* ⟵

O Father, save me from looking for matters to criticize rather than those I can commend. Help me develop the kind of eye that is quick to spot things that can be praised and slow to see those that cannot be commended. In Christ's Name. Amen.

House repairs!

"Above the Horse Gate, the priests made repairs, each in front of his own house." (v.28)

For reading & meditation – Nehemiah 3:28–32

*W*e looked the other day at a phrase which occurs several times in this third chapter – "next to." Another phrase that is repeated in the section we are looking at today is "in front of" or "opposite." In order to avoid people having to commute to their work from different parts of the city – a procedure which would have wasted time and reduced efficiency – Nehemiah arranged for each worker to build near his own home. This served two additional purposes: first, it relieved the men of unnecessary anxiety in the event of an attack (they would want to be close to their families), and second, it gave them a deep sense of family closeness as they were building.

Nehemiah knew that the home was of prime importance. This is where every real work of God must begin and be anchored. An alarming trend in today's society is the rapid disappearance of the distinctively Christian home. I refer not so much to the home where Christ resides, but to the home where Christ rules and where biblical principles prevail. Such homes are becoming hard to find.

Permit me to ask you: What are the walls like around your home? Not the physical walls but the spiritual ones – the walls of prayer, the family altar, integrity, faithfulness, openness, and so on? "The greatest test of a Christian," it has been said, "is: 'What is that person like at home?'" Before you have another meal with your family, commit yourself to undertaking any spiritual repairs that may be needed in your house. And let Christ be the Head of your home. He can do more with it than you.

FURTHER STUDY

Eph. 5:22–6:4;
2 Tim. 1:3–9;
1 Pet. 3:1–7

1. Use these passages to audit your relationships at home.

2. If you live on your own, pray for families you know.

Prayer

O Father, I want my home to be Your home. Help me rebuild any walls that may be broken down in my family life, beginning with my own personal commitment and dedication to You. This I do now. In Your Son's most precious Name. Amen.

A leader's knack

*"... between the room above the corner and the Sheep Gate the
goldsmiths and merchants made repairs." (v.32)*

For reading & meditation – Nehemiah 3:28–32

*L*ong before "management seminars" were in vogue
Nehemiah employed the principles which today's
experts claim are essential if one is to be a good and
inspiring leader. He coordinated the efforts of the workers,
inspired their cooperation by setting before them a clear vision,
and commended them for their sacrificial efforts. However, there
is one more principle that has to be considered, the fourth in the
list of good management principles: communication. This
involves the instruction of each worker so that he or she knows
what to do and where to do it. It also involves the delegation of
authority so that decisions do not need to be constantly referred to
the top.

Groups of workers had section heads. For example, "repairs
were made by the Levites under Rehum" (3:17). Nehemiah
coordinated activities by dividing the wall into about forty sections,
and each person was assigned a section of the wall. By breaking up
the project in this way Nehemiah was able to supervise the work
and communicate with one section at a time. A formidable task
becomes more easily manageable when handled piecemeal. Good,
effective leaders have a knack of simplifying a difficult task. But
their ideas sound obvious only after they have been stated.

Leadership principles may be applied to whatever the Lord has
called us to do. May many reading these lines learn from
Nehemiah how to lay down their own foundation for leadership.
Here are the four principles again: coordination, cooperation,
commendation and communication. All four are required to be a
successful leader.

FURTHER STUDY

Acts 6:1–7; 15:22–33

1. What was the outcome
of good communication
in Jerusalem?

2. What effect did it have
in Antioch?

⊹—❖ *Prayer* ❖—⊹

---

*Father, I see that things work according to certain principles; they don't just
happen. Teach me the principles governing spiritual success and help me keep to
them – no matter what. In Christ's Name. Amen.*

Unbeatable and unbreakable

"Can they bring the stones back to life from those heaps of rubble – burned as they are?" (v.2)

For reading & meditation – Nehemiah 4:1–3

*W*e have already observed that whenever a work for God gets under way it is not long before Satan begins to stir up opposition. Satan will not go to war against the people of God unless there is a good reason to do so.

When Sanballat heard that the walls of Jerusalem were being rebuilt, he became incensed and said angrily: "What does this bunch of poor, feeble Jews think they are doing?" (v.2, TLB). This is followed by Tobiah's derisory and sarcastic comment: "If even a fox climbed up on it, he would break down their wall of stones!" (v.3). A wall would have to be very poorly constructed to be toppled by a fox. Sarcasm, derision and invective are some of Satan's chief weapons when attempting to discourage God's people, as I am sure you are well aware.

I wonder how many of you today, as you go about your secular tasks, will receive some carping remark about your faith from your colleagues. Or perhaps from your own family. Satan can use even our loved ones to discourage us. C.S. Lewis said in *God in the Dock*: "It's extraordinary how inconvenient it is to your family when you get up early to go to church. It doesn't matter so much if you get up early for anything else but if you get up early for church it's selfish of you, you upset the home." Some Christians think God should preserve us from such discouragement. However, His way is not to save us from it, but to save us in it. Only when we learn to accept this fact will we be unbeatable and unbreakable.

FURTHER STUDY

Acts 7:51–60; 12:1–17

1. Why do you think Stephen was not saved from his situation?

2. Why, then, was Peter saved from his?

⊷ *Prayer* ⊷

Father, help me learn that when You don't save me from something it means that You will save me in it. My soul shrinks from criticism and sarcasm but grant me the grace that makes me more than a match for even that. In Jesus' Name. Amen.

What a prayer!

"Do not cover up their guilt or blot out their sins from your sight ..." (v.5)

For reading & meditation – Nehemiah 4:4–5

Nehemiah, when faced with criticism, took the route every one of us should take when confronted with the same problem – he poured out his heart to God in prayer. And what a prayer it is! The nature of his prayer has been a source of embarrassment to Christians down the ages as it seems to fly in the face of all that the New Testament teaches concerning loving one's enemies. So why did God allow it to be recorded?

There are several different explanations. Some say the people of the Middle East are highly excitable and quick to evoke the curse of a deity on someone they dislike. This, therefore, reveals Nehemiah functioning under the constraints of his carnality. Others say the teaching of grace and forgiveness toward one's enemies is a New Testament concept and should not be expected in Old Testament characters. But is this really so? Grace was taught by Moses, David and many others (see Exodus 23:4–5).

I remember asking a tutor at the college I attended why God allowed this prayer to be recorded without some kind of divine disclaimer. His reply made me think deeply: "You have to be a very spiritual person to pray that kind of prayer." The imprecatory psalms contain similar language (for example, Psalms 35, 79, 109). Nehemiah did not take action against those who opposed him but invited God to redress the wrong. Many of us when opposed might feel like praying in this fashion but usually our prayer is prompted more by a grudge at what is happening to us than grief at what is happening to the work of God.

FURTHER STUDY

Psa. 79:1–13; 83:1–18; 94:1–23; 137:1–9; Rom. 12:14–21

1. What did the psalmist plead for?

2. What does Paul teach about enemies?

⟶ *Prayer* ⟵

O Father, help me stop to consider today how much of my praying is governed more by a grudge toward others than grief at what might be happening to them – or even Your honor. In Christ's Name I pray. Amen.

Faith versus fear

"... for the people worked with all their heart." (v.6)

For reading & meditation – Nehemiah 4:6–11

*D*espite the opposition of Sanballat and Tobiah, the people, under Nehemiah's inspiring leadership, press on with the task of rebuilding the walls. Before long the wall reaches half the required height because "the people worked with all their heart." On hearing further reports about the success of Nehemiah's mission the enemies of Judah decide to wage war against Jerusalem.

What is Nehemiah's response to this disturbing news? He turns once more to prayer. This time the situation demands not only prayer but action. "We prayed to our God," he says, "and posted a guard" (v.9). There are times when prayer is enough to deal with a situation, but there are other times when prayer needs to be accompanied by action. Faith must join hands with works.

Though morale was high, the moment came when, due to the threats from Sanballat and the others, some of the people in Judah became discouraged and wanted to quit. This is rather surprizing, for the people of Judah were regarded as strong and valiant. Of them it had been written: "Your hand will be on the neck of your enemies ... You are a lion's cub ... who dares to rouse him?" (Gen. 49:8–9). They said the reason for their discouragement was physical exhaustion, but Nehemiah knew the real reason was fear. This is why he turned their attention to the Lord who is "great and awesome" (v.14). Fear can only be overcome with faith; not in oneself but faith in God. Is fear knocking at your door right now? Then, as you answer its knock, take Jesus with you. Don't be surprised if you find no one there.

FURTHER STUDY

Luke 8:49–56; James 2:14–26

1. What limits are there to combining faith and fearlessness?

2. What is the result of divorcing belief and action?

⊷ *Prayer* ⊶

Lord Jesus Christ, no fears lurked within Your heart to cripple and hinder. You had a heart that was unafraid. Give that same heart to me even now. For Your own dear Name's sake. Amen.

Armed for warfare

"Our God will fight for us!" (v.20)
For reading & meditation – Nehemiah 4:12–20

ehemiah's three-pronged counter-attack – prayer, vigilant guards and the charge to look continually to the Lord – is so successful that he writes: "We all returned to the wall, each to his own work" (v.15). However, the work proceeds at a much slower pace. Half the workforce stand on guard while the other half give themselves to the task of reconstruction. A trumpeter is ready to summon everyone in the event of a surprise attack. "Those who carried materials did their work with one hand and held a weapon in the other" (v.17).

As we seek to rebuild the walls that have been broken down either by neglect or by Satan and his forces, let us not forget that we are engaged in a battle as well as in a building prrgram. Scripture says that "the devil prowls around like a roaring lion looking for someone to devour" (1 Pet. 5:8). Again: "Our struggle is not against flesh and blood, but against the rulers, against the authorities, against the powers of this dark world" (Eph. 6:12). We must go about our task with a sword in one hand and a trowel in the other. In addition to the gifts God has given us to build His kingdom in this world, we need a sword to defend ourselves against Satan. The sword of the Spirit is the Word of God. The more we memorize the Word and meditate on it, the stronger will be our resistance to the devil and his armies.

We must be careful, however, that battling does not replace building. One must not be done at the expense of the other. The walls have to go up – no matter what.

FURTHER STUDY

1 Sam. 17:37–40;
2 Kings 6:8–17

1. Why did David confidently reject Saul's armor?

2. What is the complementary truth in 2 Kings?

—◆ *Prayer* ◆—

O God, help me not to become so taken up with aspects of spiritual warfare that I lose sight of the essential building work. Show me the task that You want me to do and enable me to get on with it even while battling against the foe. Amen.

Don't get in a rut!

"So we continued the work with half the men holding spears,
from the first light of dawn ..." (v.21)

For reading & meditation – Nehemiah 4:21–23

*T*he final verses of this chapter show that Nehemiah's encouraging words and the countermeasures he initiated have a positive effect on the people, ridding them of their weariness and despondency and galvanizing them into determined action. Not a moment of daylight is wasted as the taskforce throw themselves into activity from dawn until nightfall. These verses show us perhaps better than any others the chief reason for Nehemiah's success. He was one with the people. He was willing to endure the same privations, suffer the same hardships and face the same dangers as everyone else. Derek Kidner, in his commentary on Nehemiah, says: "He was not an egalitarian, but used his special resources to make his contribution the more effective."

Leaders today could learn a lot from studying how Nehemiah handled himself during these trying times. When a difficult situation arose he faced it objectively and confidently, believing that nothing could ever overtake him that God and he could not work out together. He was sensitive to the needs of his people as well as to the plots and schemes of those who were bent on his downfall. While he may have felt frustrated by the interruptions to his plans, he nevertheless faced each situation realistically and adjusted his plans accordingly.

The willingness to reorder our priorities whenever necessary is something we all ought to be open to, whether or not we are leaders. Those who are not willing to do this get stuck in a rut.

FURTHER STUDY

Heb. 2:9–18; 4:15–16

1. Why was Jesus made like us in every way?

2. How do we benefit from Jesus having been tempted?

⊷ *Prayer* ⊷

O God, deliver me from rigidity – the attitude of mind that hates necessary change and the reordering of things. Whatever reviews are necessary in my life, help me to rise to them in the strength that comes from You. In our Lord's Name I pray. Amen.

Rich man – poor man

"Now the men and their wives raised a great outcry against their Jewish brothers." (v.1)

For reading & meditation – Nehemiah 5:1–5

*I*n this chapter the perspective suddenly changes. Israel's enemies and the rebuilding of Jerusalem's walls take second place to a more immediate and pressing problem – internal dissention. The people were upset because of a food crisis – a famine – the effects of which were made worse by the increased number of Jews in Jerusalem. Furthermore, there was heavy taxation and exploitation. Some rich Jews were feathering their nests by loaning money at high rates of interest, arranging mortgages with oppressive terms and generally exploiting those in financial difficulty. Among those affected were laborers and others who did not own land (v.2). They were deeply discouraged because they were so short of food. Another group were farmers (v.3). They had raised money by mortgaging their fields, but as times were difficult and the rate of interest being charged was exorbitant, the "loan sharks" had come, repossessed their land and sold their families into slavery (v.5).

Of all the tensions that arise in society, the most difficult to resolve are those which exist between the rich and the poor, the affluent and the underprivileged. James wrote of this problem (see James 2:1–13), and it continues to plague society today. God had decreed that to make provision for the poor, the rich were to lend to them (Deut. 15:7–11) without charging interest (Ex. 22:25; Lev. 25:36). But these wise provisions had become a dead letter.

When we disregard any of God's rules for living as laid down in Scripture, we expose ourselves to troubles. We take His way or we take the consequences. Period.

FURTHER STUDY

Deut. 15:7–11;
James 2:1–13

1. Why is there disharmony between Deuteronomy 15:4 and 15:11?
2. What should govern our reaction to economic inequality?

→ Prayer ←

O God, open my eyes to see that when I go Your way I receive the benefits and rewards. When I go against Your way then I have to suffer the consequences. Help me take Your way in everything, dear Lord. In Jesus' Name. Amen.

When very angry

"When I heard their outcry and these charges, I was very angry." (v.6)

For reading & meditation – Nehemiah 5:6

aced with this new problem of internal dissention, how does Nehemiah react? He becomes very angry. The emotion of anger is something that affects most of us – even mature Christians. Few of us go through life without feeling angry from time to time.

Over the years I have observed that people handle anger in several different ways. Some get angry but convince themselves they are not. These people live in denial. Unacknowledged anger finds a way to leak out – sometimes into the physical system in the form of muscular or other physiological problems. Others feel anger and proceed to deal with it by dumping it on everyone in sight. Then there are some who experience anger but suppress it for a while and later take their feelings out on those they know are afraid of them. Watch how Nehemiah handles his feelings of anger. First he acknowledges them (v.6). He does not excuse his feelings or minimize them. He admits that he had been very angry. And he doesn't dump his feelings on others either. He keeps his anger under control. Then he takes time to ponder and evaluate the situation (v.7). By carefully weighing all the issues and thinking matters through, he is able to find the right strategy for dealing with the situation.

How different our lives would be if, whenever we became angry, we followed Nehemiah's example. First, acknowledge the anger. Second, choose not to allow it to get out of control. Third, carefully and prayerfully think through the best way of dealing with the situation which aroused the anger in the first place. Easier said than done? Maybe. Why don't you try it and see.

FURTHER STUDY

John 2:12–23;
Matt. 6:24;
Eph. 4:17–32

1. What circumstances justify anger?

2. How are we to prevent our anger becoming sin?

✦ *Prayer* ✦

My Father and my God, help me follow these principles the next time I feel a negative emotion, such as anger, rise within me. Impress them so deeply in my life that they will become as natural to me as breathing. For Jesus' sake. Amen.

Doing what is right

"... 'What you are doing is not right. Shouldn't you walk in the fear of our God ...?'" (v.9)

For reading & meditation – Nehemiah 5:7–11

esterday we watched Nehemiah deal with his anger in a positive and productive way. Now we watch him as he puts into action the ideas that came to him as he carefully thought through the situation.

Nehemiah knew that what was being practiced by the loan sharks went completely against God's instructions, and so he courageously confronts those in the wrong. He first confronts the hierarchy of Jerusalem privately, then calls a large meeting so that everything can be brought out into the open. Here he spells out his objections once again and challenges the nobles to return to the Lord and order their lives by the standards He has laid down. He reproaches the leaders for the fact that they have sold their own people into slavery, and they are shamed into silence when he goes on to say that the people they sold to the Gentiles have been bought back by Nehemiah and his friends. They are shamed even further when Nehemiah reproves them for not walking "in the fear of our God," and challenges them to return immediately the land, property and interest they had taken.

Sometimes more is needed than to think through issues objectively; we need courage also to face and confront those with whom we strongly disagree. Many of us, whenever we know we are right about an issue (at least in our own eyes), are content to settle for being right. Only under extreme provocation do we discuss the cause of our anger or concern with the offending party. It is all too easy to find reasons for not doing what we know needs to be done.

FURTHER STUDY

2 Kings 12:1–15;
1 Cor. 5:1–5

1. What can frustrate our good intentions?

2. When can a church take disciplinary action?

→ *Prayer* ←

My Father and my God, help me not to be complacent about issues that need to be confronted. And strengthen my resolve to deal with things that need dealing with not merely because I am provoked but because it is right to do so. In Jesus' Name. Amen.

How a day should end

"... the whole assembly said, 'Amen,' and praised the Lord." (v.13)

For reading & meditation – Nehemiah 5:12–13

*U*nder the lash of Nehemiah's strong rebuke the wealthy money-lenders recant and promise to give up their extortionate practices. Nehemiah knows human nature too well, however, to place confidence in verbal assurances and he demands a stronger commitment – an oath. We now witness all the nobles and officials swearing that they will return to the people their fields and property and no longer exact usury from them.

Here again we see a wise leader at work. Those who have been in similar situations know how easy it is for people to promise they will change but after a while forget the promise and return to their former ways. Some when challenged about the fact their behavior does not conform to their earlier commitment are quick to say: "But that is not what I understood I was agreeing to." Nehemiah was a realist and would not leave anything to chance. He asks the leaders for a formal commitment, and when they agree to take the oath, he validates their promise by a symbolic act. He shakes out the folds of his robe as a sign that God will reject the people if they fail to keep their promise.

As this is done the whole assembly responds with a loud "Amen." In Deuteronomy 27:15–26 we read that when a spiritual commitment is made the people who agree to it should respond by saying "Amen." However, in this instance not only did the people say "Amen" but they broke out in a spontaneous act of worship and praise. Thus a day that began in sorrow ends in spiritual rejoicing. But then, when wrongs are righted and God's Word is honored, it always does.

FURTHER STUDY

1 Kings 18:25–39;
Luke 24:13–35

1. What was the purpose of the events on Mount Carmel?

2. What transformed the downcast faces?

Prayer

O God our Father, help me never to come to the end of a day without righting all wrongs, forgiving all trespasses and ensuring that my life is in line with Your Word. This I ask for Your own dear Name's sake and Your eternal glory. Amen.

"The fear of the Lord"

"But out of reverence for God I did not act like that." (v.15)

For reading & meditation – Nehemiah 5:14–15

We have seen how the unity evident during the early stages of the rebuilding project was shattered by the exploitation of the poor by the rich. Their greed precipitated a major crisis. Nehemiah bravely dealt with the situation by confronting the nobles and rulers with the error of their ways. But to instruct those responsible to "Do as I say" would have resulted in disastrous consequences if his own conduct had not been above reproach. Nehemiah tells us in the verses before us today that though he held an eminent position in Judah, he never used that position to serve his own interests. "Out of reverence for God I did not act like that," he says (v.15).

Here is the dynamic that motivated the godly Nehemiah – reverence for God. Unless you and I, as Christian people, revere God, we are not going to progress very far along the spiritual path. Reverence for the Lord is described in Scripture as the foundation of right conduct (Psa. 111:10; Prov. 1:7). Underlying "reverence for God" or, as some translations put it, "the fear of the Lord," is holiness. No one can ascend the hill of the Lord unless he has clean hands and a pure heart (Psa. 24:3–4). And "without holiness no one will see the Lord" (Heb. 12:14).

In an age when standards are being lowered and moral absolutes ignored, it is so easy to rationalize issues and cut corners morally on the basis that everyone else is doing the same. But blessed are those who, like Nehemiah, stand up for truth and righteousness and say: "But out of reverence for God I did not act like that."

FURTHER STUDY

Gen. 22:1–18;
Matt. 3:13–17

1. What was the outcome of Abraham's willingness to revere God?

2. What resulted from Jesus' determination to honor God?

✦ Prayer ✦

O God, give me today a fresh vision of Your holiness so that I truly understand what it means to revere You and live in awe of You. And may that reverence show itself in all I do and say. For Jesus' sake. Amen.

Saying "yes"

"Remember me with favor, O my God, for all I have done for these people." (v.19)

For reading & meditation – Nehemiah 5:16–19

DAY
92

"T he secret of success in the Christian life," I was once told by an old and godly pastor, "is not just saying 'No' to whatever is wrong, but saying 'Yes' to what is right." Yesterday we saw how Nehemiah said "No" to wrongdoing; today we see how he said "Yes" to God's plans. "I devoted myself to the work on this wall," he tells us (v.16). More is required of us as Christians than turning our backs on that which is negative; we must also turn our faces toward the positive – the will and purpose of God.

Nehemiah's decision to devote himself to rebuilding the wall instead of developing an affluent lifestyle shows him to have been purposeful and committed to one task. He did not get caught up with private ventures or peripheral issues with their distractions. Instead he concentrated on one thing only. The charge of pursuing conflicting interests could not be laid at his door. Even his servants worked shoulder to shoulder with the rest of the people.

From Nehemiah's example another important principle emerges – single-mindedness. Whatever we are called to do for God, we will not experience success unless we are single-minded. It is so easy to be sidetracked by some other "worthy" cause and get caught up in pursuing things that, though good in themselves, prevent us from giving all our energies to the one thing we are called to do. Sometimes the good has to be disregarded in order to achieve the best. Nehemiah's prayer here provides us with one more insight into his modus operandi. He did nothing important without lifting his heart to God in prayer. Neither should we.

FURTHER STUDY

Matt. 21:28–32;
Phil. 3:7–14

1. What results from saying "Yes" but not acting on it?

2. What is the goal of Christian single-mindedness?

⊷ *Prayer* ⊶

Gracious and loving Father, give me a prayerful heart – a heart that lifts itself to You as naturally and as effortlessly as a feather is carried by the breeze. Deepen my dependence – my awareness of my need of You. In Jesus' Name. Amen.

A trap of the devil

"I am carrying on a great project and cannot go down." (v.3)

For reading & meditation – Nehemiah 6:1–4

*A*t last, despite enormous difficulties, the task of rebuilding the walls surrounding Jerusalem is completed. The doors in the gateways have yet to be put in place, but this, compared to the work on the walls, is a comparatively small matter.

When Sanballat, Tobiah and Geshem receive the news that Jerusalem's walls have been rebuilt they are incensed and decide to attack Nehemiah personally. They send a message to him saying: "Come, let us meet ... on the plain of Ono" (v.2). Nehemiah knew they were planning to harm him and, even though they send the same message four times, his answer always remained the same: "I am doing a great work! Why should I stop to come and visit you?" (v.3, TLB). Nehemiah knew also that leaving Jerusalem at this crucial time would mean the people were without adequate leadership and might soon lapse into their old ways. Nehemiah's place was in Jerusalem, and nothing would draw him away.

There are times when the temptation that came to Nehemiah comes also to those seeking to do something special for God. It is the temptation to give up what we are doing in the interest of tact. I know the sharpness of that temptation and I am sure many of you do too. The devil steps up to us and whispers: "Stop what you are doing and explain your actions to others. Diplomacy and dialogue will help you get your work done faster." There may be a place for diplomacy and dialogue, but the situation must be evaluated most carefully. Sometimes the suggestion can be a trap of the devil – a device calculated to divert you from your God-given task.

FURTHER STUDY

**Luke 4:1–13;
1 Pet. 5:6–11**

1. What 3 steps did Jesus take to repel the devil?

2. What 4 steps must we take to resist him?

Prayer

O God, help me be aware of every attempt the devil makes to divert me from the work You have called me to do. May I be willing to listen to others but always obedient to You. In Christ's Name. Amen.

Quiet confidence

"But I prayed, 'Now strengthen my hands.'" (v.9)
For reading & meditation – Nehemiah 6:5–9

Having again failed to achieve their purpose by intrigue, Sanballat and his co-conspirators try a new approach – innuendo. Sanballat sends an open letter to Nehemiah accusing him of plotting a rebellion against King Artaxerxes. An open letter is the height of indignity. Sanballat is aware that the letter will be made known to the public at large and that the implication of treason may well question Nehemiah's character and undermine his influence. This attack on Nehemiah exploited a well-known quirk in the human personality, namely our willingness to believe the worst about others. Think how quickly scandal runs through an office, an organization or even a church. With the faintest hint of indiscreet behavior the person concerned is soon labelled "guilty."

The suggestion that Nehemiah was involved in treasonous activities was really a form of blackmail. Such a scheme can succeed only when the person against whom it is levelled is prone to fear. Nehemiah rebuts the attack with a definite denial and once again turns to prayer. There are only two options when we find ourselves in the position where, like Nehemiah, we are openly and falsely accused and our motives maligned. One is open denial and the other, earnest prayer. What did the godly Nehemiah pray for? That the accusations would carry no weight with the people? No, he prayed that his hands might be strengthened so that the work might prosper. He was happy to leave his reputation and future to the One he served. That's quiet confidence – the kind, if we know Nehemiah's God, we can have too.

FURTHER STUDY

Gen. 39:1–23;
2 Tim. 1:7–12

1. What was the secret of Joseph's confidence in God?

2. What were the grounds of Paul's confidence?

→ *Prayer* ←

Gracious and loving heavenly Father, forgive me that under the pressure of false accusations I so easily fall apart. Help me to know You in the way that Nehemiah knew You so that I may have that same confidence too. In Jesus' Name I pray. Amen.

Outwitted, outmaneuvered

"Remember Tobiah and Sanballat, O my God, because of what they have done ..." (v.14)

For reading & meditation – Nehemiah 6:10–14

As the final stage of the building program is being completed – the installation of the gates – Nehemiah visits the house of Shemaiah. Shemaiah tries to convince Nehemiah that his life is in danger because men are coming to kill him and that they must both flee to the Temple. Since Shemaiah had access to the Temple he may have been a priest. The term used for the Temple refers to the Holy Place – which only the priests were permitted to enter.

Nehemiah's reply is blunt: "Should a man like me run away? Or should one like me go into the temple to save his life?" (v.11). He senses that Shemaiah is not a true ambassador of God but rather an agent hired by Sanballat and Tobiah. He senses, too, that the plot to get him into the Temple is an attempt to discredit him. If Nehemiah had gone with Shemaiah into the Holy Place, he would have laid himself open to two charges: cowardice and the violation of the law that permitted only priests to stand in that Holy Place.

Nehemiah's encounter with Shemaiah leaves him with a deep sense of his vulnerability. Once again his heart turns to the Lord in prayer. Nehemiah knows that his life and reputation have been preserved not by breaking God's laws but by keeping them. When we do what is right, we can safely leave all the consequences with God. "No weapon forged against you will prevail" is how Isaiah puts it (Isa. 54:17). I think the Lord wants me to tell someone that this word of Isaiah's is His special one for you today. Take it to heart and be encouraged.

FURTHER STUDY

Josh. 2:1–15;
Acts 9:20–30

1. Why was Rahab right to help the spies escape?

2. Why was Saul right to outwit his enemies?

↦ Prayer ↤

O Father, how can I sufficiently thank You for reminding me that when I do right then I can safely leave all the consequences of my action with You? You are able to outmaneuver everybody and everything. My heart rejoices in You. Amen.

The importance of prayer

"So the wall was completed on the twenty-fifth of Elul, in fifty-two days." (v.15)

For reading & meditation – Nehemiah 6:15–19

T he whole job of rebuilding the wall and putting the gates in place took, we are told, just fifty-two days – a remarkable accomplishment. When those who had opposed Nehemiah's work hear of his success they lose some of their self-confidence because they realize that such a project could never have been accomplished without God's help. But even with such irrefutable evidence of the hand of God at work, it becomes clear from today's section that enemies were still plotting – both within and outside Jerusalem. Tobiah the Ammonite, by reason of the fact that he had married a Jewess (the daughter of Shecaniah), had many relatives in Jerusalem. His son had followed his example and also married a Jewess, the daughter of Meshullam (v.18), which meant that between them they had several contacts in the city. Letters are sent to and fro between the nobles of Judah and Tobiah. Tobiah's good actions are reported to Nehemiah and Nehemiah's activities are reported to Tobiah. Threats and innuendoes continue as Tobiah seeks to intimidate Nehemiah and wear down his resilience.

The last few sentences of this chapter lead us once again to see what a spiritual stalwart Nehemiah was. Despite all the pressures he was under, he still maintained his confidence in God. A man of lesser ability and character would have given up. It has been said: "A man has no more character than is revealed when he is in a crisis." We must never forget that the foundation of spiritual success is our personal character. Whatever else we may have, if we don't have character it amounts to little or nothing.

FURTHER STUDY

Dan. 1:1–20; 3:1–28;
Acts 27:13–44

1. What gave the Hebrew young men their strength of character?

2. What effect did Paul's character have in a crisis?

⟿ *Prayer* ⟻

Gracious Father, so that I am ready for the moment of crisis, deposit within me the lineaments of Your own character. May the beauty of Jesus be seen in me – no matter what. In Jesus' Name I ask it. Amen.

Gains must be guarded

*"... Hananiah ... was a man of integrity and feared
God more than most men do." (v.2)*

For reading & meditation – Nehemiah 7:1–3

The book of Nehemiah falls naturally into two parts. The first six chapters deal with the reconstruction of Jerusalem's walls; the last seven chapters with the re-instruction of the people.

As Nehemiah initiates "Phase Two," he selects reliable men to whom he can delegate important responsibilities. The first appointee is his own brother Hanani, whom he creates governor of Jerusalem. Was Nehemiah guilty of nepotism in selecting his own brother for this honor? No, for in Hanani he saw a man who was concerned for others. It was Hanani, you remember, who brought Nehemiah the news that Jerusalem's walls were in ruins (1:2–3). Alongside Hanani a man with a similar name – Hananiah – is appointed to be commander of the citadel. He too is regarded by Nehemiah as a man of integrity, and we are told that he "feared God more than most men do." These men with their strong commitment to the Lord were sorely needed with traitorous Jews in high places and leading families involved in intrigue. Then, having ensured that certain residents will act as watchmen, Nehemiah gives Hanani and Hananiah instructions on how to safeguard the city.

It is always a mistake to think that because spiritual objectives have been reached nothing more needs to be done. Gains must be guarded. Times of great spiritual achievement can be as dangerous as times of disappointment if they put us off our guard. Vigilance is required of us at all times.

FURTHER STUDY

Matt. 25:1–13;
1 Tim. 6:11–21

1. What is the likely consequence of lack of spiritual vigilance?

2. How can spiritual alertness be maintained?

❧ *Prayer* ❧

My Lord and my God, help me to be always vigilant. Help me also to understand that being constantly vigilant does not mean that I can never relax, but rather that I do not relinquish a sense of spiritual alertness. In Jesus' Name I pray. Amen.

Taking stock of the past

"So my God put it into my heart to assemble [the people] for registration by families." (v.5)

For reading & meditation – Nehemiah 7:4–38

Following the appointment of new leaders for the city, Nehemiah is prompted by the Lord to register the people and consult the genealogical record of the exiles who had returned under Zerubbabel. Yet again we see how close a relationship Nehemiah had with the Lord. Note the words: "So my God put it into my heart." In every chapter so far we have witnessed him talking to God or God talking to him. He illustrates perhaps more than any other biblical character what it means to "practice the presence of God."

The purpose of the census is to determine the genealogical purity of the people and of the priesthood in anticipation of the repopulation of the city. The long list of names which forms most of this chapter makes it difficult to analyze it section by section. It is a bridge between the first six chapters and the final six. The first six chapters record how Nehemiah accomplished his primary goal – the rebuilding of the wall. The last six chapters (8–13) record how the work of consolidation was carried out. Chapter 7 is transitional and records the first step toward the consolidation of the work. Before the people can enter into all that God has for them, they must be sure of their inheritance and their calling.

The same is true of us also. We need to know exactly what we have inherited in Christ if we are to enter into it. And what have we inherited? Life, peace, power, joy – riches beyond compare. It is one thing, however, to know of our inheritance. It is another to enter into it.

FURTHER STUDY

Deut. 8:2–5;
Gal. 3:22–4:7

1. What can be learned from the past?

2. What is the one condition for entering into our inheritance?

⊷ *Prayer* ⊶

My Father, take me by the hand and lead me to all the riches that are available to me in Christ. Forgive me that I put up with spiritual poverty when so much is mine. Help me not merely to acknowledge my inheritance but appropriate it. In Jesus' Name. Amen.

Purity in the pulpit

*"... they could not find [their family records] and so were
excluded from the priesthood as unclean." (v.64)*

For reading & meditation – Nehemiah 7:39–69

We pause in reading through this long list of names to
focus on a fact that is well worth further thought.
Here, in the section before us today, we see listed a
group of people who were unable to show that their families had
descended from Israel, and among whom were a company of
priests. These priests, because they could not prove their spiritual
pedigree, were summarily dismissed from the priesthood.

This might seem an extreme measure, especially as they had
participated for some time in the activities connected with worship
and had gained great experience in that ministry. But there is no
room for sentiment when it comes to God's instructions. A pure
and proper priesthood was essential if the people were to maintain
a right relationship with the Lord. We must never forget that it is
spirituality, not sentiment, that is the foundation of service for
God. The danger facing Israel when the priesthood was not in
accordance with God's requirements was a very serious one
indeed.

The point is not without its parallel today. Some being ordained
into the ministry nowadays are unable to prove their spiritual
birth. They do not know what it means to be "saved." And they
label those who say they are as either spiritually naive or arrogant.
How I wish the leaders of some denominations were as faithful to
the Word of God as was Nehemiah and would exclude from such
a sacred place as the pulpit those who have no clear spiritual
testimony. Only those who have experienced the saving grace of
Christ can hope to minister that grace to others.

FURTHER STUDY

2 Kings 22:1–13;
Heb. 5:1–14

1. How did Josiah react
to the words he heard?

2. What condition is laid
down in Hebrews for
ministers?

⊷ *Prayer* ⊶

*O God my Father, I see how easily the spiritual life of Your Church can be
hindered when there is no purity in the pulpit. Give us men like Nehemiah who
will help preserve our spiritual purity. In Christ's Name I pray. Amen.*

No sacrifice - no hope

*"Some of the heads of the families contributed
to the work." (v.70)*

For reading & meditation – Nehemiah 7:70–73

*T*his final section of chapter 7 shows how following the exclusion of the priests a spirit of liberality seemed to break out. People willingly gave to the Lord's work and heading the list, the record says, were "some of the heads of the families." A number of commentators think the "heads of the families" had hitherto been overshadowed by other more prominent people (the rulers, for example), but here those who acted as "shepherds of the families" receive special mention. What greater distinction can anyone have than to lead and guide a family into a closer and deeper relationship with the Lord? They gave willingly to the work of the Temple and their generous giving set an example which others quickly followed.

How wonderful it is when God's people take seriously the work of the ministry and give sacrificially for its support. I know churches whose ministers have had to take secular employment in order to support themselves because even though there were enough financially sound people in the congregation to underwrite their living, they did not have a heart to give. Such situations are a blot on the reputation of the Church and on the Name of our Lord Jesus Christ. Generosity generates generosity, and when people open their purse strings and give liberally to God's work great things happen.

One of the precursors to spiritual blessing in a church is the congregation's desire to show respect for the work of the ministry. I do not hesitate to say that where there is no sacrifice in a congregation there is no hope for a congregation.

FURTHER STUDY

**Mark 12:41–44;
1 Cor. 9:1–18**

1. How did Jesus turn accepted values upside down?

2. How did Paul qualify his claim for support?

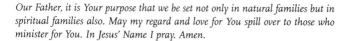

─── ✦ *Prayer* ✦ ───

Our Father, it is Your purpose that we be set not only in natural families but in spiritual families also. May my regard and love for You spill over to those who minister for You. In Jesus' Name I pray. Amen.

Hungry for the Word!

*"And all the people listened attentively to the
Book of the Law." (v.3)*

For reading & meditation – Nehemiah 8:1–4

*O*nce the great task of the rebuilding of the wall and the census has been completed, Nehemiah fades into the background for a while and Ezra the scribe comes into the spotlight. Though he had been sent to Jerusalem some thirteen years earlier he was not eager for personal glory, and so remained in the background, only coming forward when he was asked to read from the Scripture.

It is now the seventh month, the most solemn month of the year, ushered in by the Feast of Trumpets. So universal is the spiritual awakening that the people leave their towns and make their way to Jerusalem "as one man" to hear Ezra read the Scriptures to them. Just think of that: Ezra did not need to call on the people to get them to hearken to the reading of God's Word – they called upon him. The scribe, accompanied by thirteen priests, ascends the wooden platform built specially for this purpose by the Water Gate and begins to read from the Word. The reading and explanation took five or six hours, during which everyone listened attentively. As a consequence of such eagerness to listen to the Word of God something significant was bound to happen.

A person once said to me: "Wouldn't it be wonderful if we had expositors like Ezra who could hold people's attention for several hours?" My reply was this: "Yes, but wouldn't it be wonderful also if we had congregations eager enough to want to listen to the Word of God being expounded for several hours!" When those who love to expound the Word and those who love hearing the Word expounded meet, then anything can happen.

FURTHER STUDY

Matt. 15:29–39;
Acts 17:10–15

1. Why did Jesus need to feed the crowd?

2. What can be the consequence of faithful preaching?

◆ *Prayer* ◆

O God, forgive us if our souls are easily satisfied and we have lost the hunger to hear Your Word. Bring Your Church to the place where Your people were in Nehemiah's day, we pray. No matter what it costs. In Jesus' Name. Amen.

Back to the Bible!

"They read from the Book of the Law of God, making it clear and giving the meaning ..." (v.8)

For reading & meditation – Nehemiah 8:5–8

We saw yesterday that the reading and exposition of the Scriptures given by Ezra lasted from daybreak until noon – a period of five or six hours. How much of Scripture would he have covered in that time? No doubt quite a lot, even allowing for the fact that he paused to explain the readings.

As soon as Ezra opened up the Book of the Law and praised the Lord, all the people stood up, lifted up their hands to heaven and said "Amen," which means "So be it." "Then they bowed down and worshipped the Lord with their faces to the ground" (v.6). This was not the practice of bibliolatry – the worship of a book. The praise and adoration was for God and in anticipation of what they were to hear from His Word.

Wouldn't it be wonderful if the opening of God's Word brought such an enthusiastic response from God's people today? The point we need to get hold of from the passage we are reflecting on is this: it is not enough to hear the Word of God; it must also be carefully explained. That is why God has gifted certain people in the Church to explain the Scriptures. When the great nineteenth-century Baptist preacher C. H. Spurgeon first came to London, he noticed that the people who attended his church were so starved spiritually that even a morsel of biblical exposition was a treat to them. By the time he completed his ministry it was said that his people knew more of the Bible than many a theologian. Today churches tend to emphasise experience rather than Bible exposition. People languish where the Word of God is not explained.

FURTHER STUDY

Psa. 1:1–6;
2 Tim. 2:1–15

1. What must a preacher do to be effective?
2. What guidelines does Paul lay down?

⊶ *Prayer* ⊷

O God, help us as Your people to put the Bible back in its proper place. Forgive us that we have allowed it to be displaced by other things. Raise up strong teachers to teach us and challenge us. For Your own dear Name's sake. Amen.

Don't mourn too long

"Do not grieve, for the joy of the Lord is your strength." (v.10)

For reading & meditation – Nehemiah 8:9–12

Clearly the reading and exposition of God's Word has a profound effect upon the people. The truths of Scripture fly like arrows into their hearts producing deep spiritual conviction, and they weep. It is a good thing to weep before the Lord whenever we feel convicted of sin, but it is possible to become overly absorbed with our failures and thus spend too much time mourning over our sins. Mourning can lead to self-contempt if we allow it to go on too long. And self-contempt is more a human than a spiritual dynamic. Though mourning over our sins is right we must remember that it is not our mourning that takes away our sin; rather, it is the redemption which God has procured for us in Christ Jesus.

Nehemiah, Ezra and the Levites encourage the people to spend the rest of the day feasting and sharing their food with those who have nothing prepared. This instruction moves them from being too introspective and self-centerd to being outgoing and other-centerd. Other-centerdness is always a good sign that God is at work in our hearts.

Nehemiah then reminds the people that the joy of the Lord is their strength. This statement puts the whole matter into perspective. I have known people who have mourned over their sins, but afterwards a sense of failure has still remained. Weeping ought to bring us to the end of our own resources so that we might discover our strength in the Lord. What greater strength is there than in joy? What greater joy is there than the joy of sins forgiven? We can live for God's glory only when we live in this kind of joy.

FURTHER STUDY

John 6:66–69;
Phil. 4:4–13

1. What puts everything in its true perspective?

2. What does joy bring about?

⤞ *Prayer* ⤝

O my Father, I see that joy is a simple, natural, spontaneous delight based on a right relationship to God, to others and myself. Help me to take my birthright of joy and live the life for which I am made. In Christ's Name. Amen.

Into the Word - daily

*"... the heads of all the families ... gathered round Ezra ...
to give attention to the words of the Law." (v.13)*

For reading & meditation – Nehemiah 8:13–18

However spiritually exciting things might appear, what we are experiencing is not a true movement of the Spirit unless it affects our wills. The spiritual renewal described in this chapter began with the people's expectation, developed through the exposition of the Word, and moved on to touch the emotions. If it had ended there – with the emotions – then I doubt whether we would be reading about it at this moment.

In the section before us today we see how the spiritual movement that began in the five- or six-hour meeting culminates in the people desiring to know and do the will of the Lord. It is now the day following what might be described as "the day of renewal," and the heads of the families meet with Ezra for more instruction from the Word. As Ezra reads to them, they find they have not kept the Feast of Tabernacles which, according to the instructions God gave to Moses, should take place during the seventh month. The Feast of Tabernacles commemorated the Exodus and reminded the Jews of the wandering of their fathers in the desert, when God made the people "live in booths" (Lev. 23:43). Once they realize their oversight, they determine to keep the feast at once. This reveals their willingness to submit to the Word of God and do as it commands – not just to hear it.

So great is their longing to know more of God's Word that Ezra is asked to hold daily Bible studies. One day of teaching is not enough for these people – they want instruction on a regular basis. With such spiritual hunger, is it any wonder revival is in the air?

FURTHER STUDY

Deut. 4:1–9;
Matt. 7:24–29

1. What is promised to those who hear and then do?

2. What happens to people who hear but fail to act?

⊷⊷ *Prayer* ⊷⊷

Father, whatever work of the Spirit goes on in my heart, may it have its effect not merely in my emotions but in my will also. I do not simply want to feel good; I want to be good – to obey You in all I do. Help me ever to do this. In Christ's Name. Amen.

What galvanizes?

"They stood in their places and confessed their sins and the wickedness of their fathers." (v.2)

For reading & meditation – Nehemiah 9:1–5

For the last two days we have had a picture of a great crowd of happy people feasting and enjoying the presence of the Lord. Now we see the same people going without food, dressed in sackcloth and with dust on their heads. What has gone wrong? Has some awful sin been uncovered?

No, they are giving evidence of their contrition. Their fasting bears witness to their devotion, the sackcloth symbolizes their inner repentance, and the dust on their heads is the external sign of the sorrow they feel in their hearts. In view of the fact that this is a solemn convocation, foreigners are not allowed to join in. For three hours they stand confessing their sins and listening to the Word of God, and for a further three hours they worship the Lord. After this preparation the people are ready to be led in prayer. It seems that during the time of worship they have been in a kneeling position as the Levites instruct them to "Stand up and praise the Lord."

What an impressive sight this is. Gone is all sense of inferiority and fear. Though numerically they were much weaker than their enemies, their faith has been quickened by the things they have discovered through the reading and exposition of the Scriptures. A vastly different atmosphere would pervade our churches if only we would give more time to focusing our eyes on the Lord, listening to His Word being expounded and talking to Him in prayer. I tell you – nothing galvanizes the human spirit and rids it of negativism and inferiority more effectively than time spent in the presence of the Eternal One.

FURTHER STUDY

2 Chron. 7:1–10;
Heb. 12:18–29

1. What is the response of worshippers who see God's glory?

2. What should cause thankfulness and what should this lead to?

⇥ *Prayer* ⇤

O Father, forgive us that we spend a greater amount of time exposing our spirits to the world than we do to You. I see that to become more like You I must spend more time with You. Help us to do that both individually and corporately. In Jesus' Name.

The God-focus

"Blessed be your glorious name, and may it be exalted ..." (v.5)
For reading & meditation – Nehemiah 9:5–15

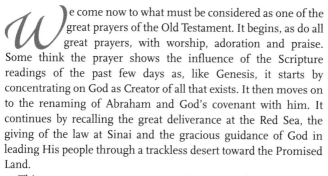

e come now to what must be considered as one of the great prayers of the Old Testament. It begins, as do all great prayers, with worship, adoration and praise. Some think the prayer shows the influence of the Scripture readings of the past few days as, like Genesis, it starts by concentrating on God as Creator of all that exists. It then moves on to the renaming of Abraham and God's covenant with him. It continues by recalling the great deliverance at the Red Sea, the giving of the law at Sinai and the gracious guidance of God in leading His people through a trackless desert toward the Promised Land.

This prayer, as we can see at once, is a prayer that is grounded in Scripture. If we are to pray powerfully and deeply, then our minds must be soaked in Scripture. This seems to be a lost art nowadays. When Dr. Martyn Lloyd-Jones was pastor of Westminster Chapel, London, people said they gained as much from his prayers as they did from his sermons. "He prayed," it was said, "not only out of his heart but out of the Bible." The more our prayers are rooted in the Bible, soaked in the Bible and in harmony with the Bible, the more powerful will be our praying.

Note how many times the word "You" appears in this section of the prayer. Clearly it is shot through with a God-focus. All great praying begins by focusing on God before focusing on anything else. When He is put in His rightful place, then suddenly all other things appear in their rightful place. Try it and see.

FURTHER STUDY

1 Sam. 2:1–10;
Acts 4:23–31

1. Why did Hannah denounce proud speech?

2. On what did Peter and John base their prayer?

➤ Prayer ➤

O God, forgive me that so often I rush into Your presence talking about my needs, my wants and my concerns. Help me become more concerned with giving You glory than with getting something out of You. In Jesus' Name. Amen.

Where sin abounds ...

"They ate to the full and were well-nourished; they reveled in your great goodness." (v.25)

For reading & meditation – Nehemiah 9:16–25

*W*e saw yesterday how the first section of the prayer was dominated by the word "You," referring, of course, to God. In this section the word "they" becomes prominent and alternates with "You" as the interaction of the two parties – God and the Israelites – is traced. Over and over again, like the beat of a drum, the word "they" sounds out to remind the Israelites of their forefathers' stubbornness and sinfulness: "they became arrogant ...," "they refused to listen ...," "they became stiff-necked ...," and so on.

But the main focus of this part of the prayer is not on the sinfulness of the people but the marvelous mercy and forgiving grace of God. Where sin abounds, grace superabounds. Though Israel rebelled and chose to return to slavery in Egypt, the Lord stood by His people. Even when they made a golden calf and worshipped it, He did not desert them (v.18), but continued to guide and protect them and provide everything they needed. Look at the way in which the words "You" and "they" are set against each other in describing the faithfulness of God and the stubbornness and recalcitrance of the people. God is faithful; the people unfaithful. God is consistent; the people are inconsistent. God is reliable; the people unreliable.

As the Jews listen to this powerful prayer and the contrasts it presents, they have occasion to reflect on how much more faithful God is to His people than they are to Him. Who could blame Him if He abandoned us? But how wonderful it is that He does not.

FURTHER STUDY

**Hosea 2:2–23;
Rom. 5:12–21**

1. What is God's response to His people's forgetfulness?

2. What were the different consequences of one man's sin and the trespasses of many?

⟶ *Prayer* ⟵

O God, how grateful we ought to be as Your children that in grace You do not give us up when our motives are mixed and our behavior petulant and peevish. Yet how sad that we take Your grace for granted. Forgive us and help us, dear Lord. In Jesus' Name. Amen.

Devout realists

*"But in your great mercy you did not put an end
to them or abandon them ..." (v.31)*

For reading & meditation – Nehemiah 9:26–31

The confession and acknowledgement of God's goodness continues by considering the time when the Israelites first settled in Canaan – the period of the judges – and the monarchy. Throughout these years the same pattern repeated itself over and over again – disobedience led to warnings, which when ignored resulted in punishment. In turn this led to repentance and appeals to God for mercy. Once more the words "You" and "they" draw attention to the interaction between God and His people.

This review of their national history provides every one of the Jews listening with encouraging evidences of what God has done in the past, the awesome consequences of ingratitude and the inevitability of punishment if sin goes unconfessed. But most important of all, there is hope for the future. And that hope is based on the unchanging character of God. They see in the present a product of the past and the seed of the future. Their anticipation now is that the knowledge of past events will help them avoid the evil and follow the good, which is Paul's message in 1 Corinthians 10:6 and 11.

One person has said: "We have no light to illuminate the pathway of the future save that which falls over our shoulder from the past." Reflecting on what God has done for us in the past enables us to have a clearer perspective on the present and the future. A biblical approach to history makes us neither wide-eyed optimists nor downhearted pessimists. We become devout realists, for we see God at work in all things and triumphing over everything.

FURTHER STUDY

**Psa. 23:1–6;
Luke 22:35–38**

1. As you read the psalm, reflect on God's dealings with you.

2. How will devout realists react to different situations?

⊷ *Prayer* ⊷

O God, help me build into my life times for reflection on the way in which Your goodness has been with me in the past. For I see that by contemplating this I draw hope and encouragement for the future. Answer my prayer. In Jesus' Name. Amen.

"I was wrong"

"... you have acted faithfully, while we did wrong." (v.33)

For reading & meditation – Nehemiah 9:32–37

The corporate prayer of repentance offered by the Jews now comes to the only petition: that God will have mercy and not think lightly of their hardships. But first they remind God that He is a covenant-keeping God, and then they acknowledge that He has always acted justly and been faithful to them. Next they confess their sin to Him in the words "we did wrong." I once heard a famous American preacher claim that "the three hardest words to say in all the world are 'I was wrong'." Yet here the Jewish people are saying just that: "we were wrong."

True repentance always involves an admission of wrongdoing – without excuses. If we try to excuse ourselves by admitting, "Lord, I know I was wrong in doing this, but I was a little unbalanced at the time because of all the pressures on me," we are not truly repenting. Repentance offers no excuses, indulges in no prevarications or rationalizations. We live in a day when people are quick to excuse themselves for their unacceptable behavior by pleading: "I've been hurt too so you can't expect me to behave properly under such circumstances. It's my parents fault because they gave me a negative self-image. You can't blame me for the way I act." Whatever you do, don't adopt this attitude when you come to God. Every one of us is culpable before Him. We have sinned because we like sinning. We have hurt Him because we wanted to hurt Him. So let there be no excuses when we seek forgiveness from Him. Say those three little words – "I was wrong" – and cleansing will come hard on the heels of your confession.

FURTHER STUDY

2 Sam. 12:1–13;
Psa. 32:3–5

1. What sin was David guilty of besides murder?

2. What does he say about confession in the psalm?

⊷ Prayer ⊷

O God, help me to take this truth – that confession of sin must contain no excuses for sin – and apply it to my life the next time I need to repent. I ask this in and through the peerless and precious Name of Jesus. Amen.

Making a commitment

"Those who sealed it were: Nehemiah the governor ..." (10:1)
For reading & meditation – Nehemiah 9:38; 10:1–27

The importance of making a binding agreement that commits oneself to a deeper relationship with God is something every one of us ought to understand and, whenever necessary, put into operation. Whatever words we use to describe it – dedication, consecration, covenant – the decision to commit oneself following confession of sin or when new challenges are being opened up by the Lord is an essential aspect of effective Christian living.

Clearly, as a result of the exposition of Scripture and the powerful prayer of confession, the people under the leadership of Ezra and Nehemiah decided to conserve the spiritual gains by entering into a covenant (or agreement) with their covenant-keeping God. The covenant, which presumably was drawn up by Ezra the scribe, having been accepted by the national dignitaries, was now signed and sealed by them. First to set his seal to it was Nehemiah, next Zedekiah and the other priests, the Levites and representatives of all the people. Note that in the list is the name of Shemaiah (v.8). Some think this is the person who earlier "sold out" to Sanballat and Tobiah. If so, it suggests he had come to a place of repentance and renewed commitment – a significant and welcome step forward.

The scene must have been one of the most moving ever witnessed in Israel's history as the leading people stood in line to sign and seal the covenant committing them to keeping the Lord's commandments. This kind of commitment arises from one thing only – the clear and anointed exposition of the Scriptures. Great things happen under such preaching of God's Word.

FURTHER STUDY

Josh. 24:14–27;
Luke 19:1–10

1. How did Joshua challenge the people to prove their commitment?

2. How did Zacchaeus demonstrate his commitment?

Prayer

Father, I see that I too in times of spiritual crisis need to make a deep and dedicated commitment. When I do, help me not to give half of myself, for then I will be a half-person. How can I offer to You anything else but the whole? Amen.

"Most" is not enough

"... all these now ... bind themselves with a curse and an oath to follow the Law of God ..." (v.29)

For reading & meditation – Nehemiah 10:28–31

Nehemiah now focuses on the covenant itself. The first point is the need to submit to the authority of God's laws given in the Scriptures. The people know that they cannot expect God's blessing without being obedient to Him. They also realize that they have to act responsibly before Him, and that to pray and expect God's blessing and then go one's own way just will not work. Their history has shown them the result of such foolish thinking. Disobedience has brought them the punishment that God promises He will inflict when His people wander from His path. Having suffered so much, the people now want to return to Him and stay under His blessing. Their first commitment is the commitment to uphold all that is in God's Word.

From this general commitment the people go on to make more specific ones. First, they agree to abstain from intermarriage. This had always been a problem in Israel's history, but now they recognize that marriage to those who do not hold sacred things important creates great difficulties in a home. Spiritual differences result in the children being improperly instructed in the ways of the Lord, and this in turn undermines society. Next they commit themselves to keeping the Sabbath, and every seventh year allowing the ground to lie fallow and cancelling all debts. Note the attention to detail in this covenant. Not one matter is left unidentified. Let us remember that when we commit ourselves to obeying the commandments of the Lord we must commit ourselves to obeying all of them. "Some" or "most" is not enough.

FURTHER STUDY

Acts 5:1–11;
Num. 32:23;
James 2:10–11

1. Why were Ananias and Sapphira punished?

2. What does James say about keeping God's commandments?

⋆⇒ *Prayer* ⇐⋆

O God, help me understand that though Your commandments call me up to almost unbelievable heights of conduct, through Your Spirit You empower me to reach up to them. And not just some or most, but all. I am so deeply thankful. Amen.

Worship is central

"We will not neglect the house of our God." (v.39)

For reading & meditation – Nehemiah 10:32–39

The final terms of the covenant sealed by the people have to do with maintaining the Temple and those who minister in it. This implies that God's house is once again central to the Jews' thinking. The commitment involves an assurance that there will be an adequate supply of wood, that the firstfruits of the produce will be brought annually to the Lord, that tithes will be given, and so on. The people are agreeing that the Lord's claim on their lives will touch everything they have and own – children, cattle, produce, even the new wine and oil. Whether Ezra drafted the covenant on his own or with the help of others we cannot be sure, but clearly great care was taken to cover every area of their lives. With great solemnity the people commit themselves to maintaining the house of God.

The commitment to ensuring that the things which had to do with the Temple were not neglected, though last in order, is not to be regarded as least in importance. There is always a strong link between spirituality and social conduct (though this is denied by some), and unless the worship of God (represented by the house of God) is central, all kinds of social problems will arise. Without a strong base for worship neither the Church nor society can expect to survive.

Israel's covenant with the Lord contains important principles for the Church today. Let us yield to His will and allow Him to develop within us a love for His Word, a deep desire to do His work, and a genuine concern to minister to those who, in Christ's Name, minister to us.

FURTHER STUDY

Luke 2:13–14;
Mark 12:28–34

1. What is the biblical prescription for tackling social problems?

2. What is the first priority for Christian worship?

✦ *Prayer* ✦

O God, how wonderful it would be if today all Your people everywhere committed themselves to following You and serving You wholeheartedly. Perhaps that is too much to expect but nevertheless I do so – humbly and prayerfully. Help me. In Jesus' Name. Amen.

Urban renewal

"... the rest of the people cast lots to bring one out of every ten to live in Jerusalem ..." (v.1)

For reading & meditation – Nehemiah 11:1–19

Due to the fact that Jerusalem had only a small population, it was extremely vulnerable to attack from its enemies. The new fortifications needed men to guard them constantly, and unless something was done about the problem, the city would soon be captured by its enemies. The leaders, we are told, already live in Jerusalem, but as more people are needed if the city is to be secure, lots are cast in order to decide who will be among the 10 per cent to leave the surrounding towns and villages to live in the city. Some of the Jews, who clearly are more aware now of their spiritual heritage than ever before, volunteer to move to Jerusalem, and this evidence of patriotism and concern is obviously much appreciated by the others. Once the plans for urban renewal are set in motion, Nehemiah lists the families who are to make up the new residents. First those who are descendants of Judah, next those descended from Benjamin, then those who are priests and Levites, and finally the gatekeepers and Temple servants.

How did the influx of all these new people into Jerusalem affect those who already lived there? There appears to have been no difficulty or disruption. But we must remember that the city under Nehemiah was established upon sound biblical principles, and they were in the midst of spiritual renewal. This does not mean they had no relational problems, but because of their deep commitment to spiritual things they had the will to work through them. "Where there is a will there is often a way" it is sometimes said. Where there is God's will there is always a way.

FURTHER STUDY

Heb. 11:8–16; 13:11–14;
Rev. 21:1–11; 21:22–27;
22:1–5; 22:14

1. How do we enter God's city?

2. What will not be found there?

─────── ◆═ *Prayer* ═◆ ───────

Father, I am grateful that You not only call me to do Your will but provide me with the strength to accomplish it. You ask me to do nothing of which I am not capable – providing I respond to Your power. I am so grateful. Amen.

Judah's administration

*"The rest of the Israelites ... were in all the towns of Judah,
each on his ancestral property." (v.20)*

For reading & meditation – Nehemiah 11:20–36

The verses in this section contain a list of the towns and villages in the former territories of the tribes of Judah and Benjamin. For administrative purposes the whole province was divided into districts, as a further look at chapter 3 shows us (eg, vv. 9, 14). Although subject to Persia, the people had a great deal of control over the running of their province, and each town was represented by elders and leaders who were answerable to the priests.

This form of decentralized government was unusual at the time. Outside of Judah the general system of government was a centralized one where power was concentrated in the hands of a select few and where checks were minimal. In such a system (human nature being what it is) there is always a ready climate for intrigue and strife. However, the administration of Judah, we are told, was built on a spiritual foundation, with the honor and glory of God being of paramount importance and His justice the measure of all things.

Everyone, of course, is free to argue for the political system which most appeals to them. I have my preference and you have yours. What ought to be remembered, however, is that no political system can succeed (in the fullest sense of that word) unless it is rooted in spiritual values. A wise man said many years ago: "Righteousness exalts a nation, but sin is a disgrace to any people" (Prov. 14:34). Those sentiments may have dropped out of modern-day thinking, but they remain in the Bible. They apply with equal power still.

FURTHER STUDY

**Amos 2:6–7;
Micah 2:1–2; 3:9–11;
7:1–7; 4:2–5**

1. What charge is made against the ruling classes?

2. What is the cure for these ills?

→ Prayer ←

O God, how sad I feel sometimes when I see the failure of many of the world's leaders to give You and Your principles their rightful place. May we in Your Church nevertheless be the salt and light that You have called us to be. In Jesus' Name. Amen.

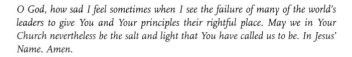

Look back to the past

"These were the priests and Levites who returned with Zerubbabel ..." (v.1)

For reading & meditation – Nehemiah 12:1–26

Many who love studying the Scriptures say that when they come to a long list of names (such as we have before us in this chapter) they move over them as quickly as they can, eager to get to the more interesting parts. But there is always a reason why names are listed in the Bible, and discovering that reason helps to sustain our interest. Here Nehemiah is concerned to identify the authentic traditions of his people. He starts with Zerubbabel, who led the first party of exiles back from Babylon ninety years earlier, and surveys the history of the priestly and Levitical families from his day onwards.

As we examine these names, we are reminded afresh of the significance of those who served the Lord before we arrived on the scene, and of the importance of godliness in the life of a nation. Many of the ordinary people may have been ignorant of their spiritual heritage. And that is always a tragedy. This is why the Bible constantly draws our attention to those who have gone before us – Hebrews 13:7 being just one example. It is largely through the labors of those who preceded us that we heard the gospel. Therefore we must resist any tendency to treat the faithful of bygone generations as being of no interest nowadays.

Unexciting as the first half of the chapter may appear, it has a point to make by its refusal to treat the people of the past as if they were no longer worth considering. History may focus on the big names, but there are lots of little names that have a big place in the heart and mind of God.

FURTHER STUDY

Isa. 51:1–2;
Heb. 11:17–40; 11:6

1. What one characteristic of God's past people must we copy?

2. What is promised to all who display this characteristic?

❧ *Prayer* ❧

Father, I look back today with thanksgiving in my heart for all those who trod this way before me. I realize that I would not belong to You now unless others had maintained the traditions of the gospel. I am grateful to them and to You. In Jesus' Name. Amen.

It's OK to be exuberant

"The sound of rejoicing in Jerusalem could be heard far away." (v.43)

For reading & meditation – Nehemiah 12:27–43

*O*nce the work of repopulating Jerusalem has been accomplished, the next great event is for the whole nation to meet and dedicate the newly rebuilt wall. For this solemn yet joyful occasion the priests and the Levites are brought to Jerusalem from wherever they live and are required to purify themselves, the people, the gates and the walls. All this is done to remind the Jews that they, and all they have, belong to the Lord in a special way.

When everything is ready for the dedication of the wall, Nehemiah divides the people and their leaders, the priests and the Levites into two groups. These groups, each led by a large choir, and with Ezra in one group and Nehemiah in the other, process around the wall in opposite directions and meet by the Temple. There, in the Temple, the choirs engage in a responsive anthem. The antiphonal choirs can be heard a great way off and everyone realizes that the music, singing and dancing mark a new day and a new beginning in the life of the nation. Some think that exuberance and devotion cannot belong together. They can. Both Jewish and Church history bears witness to this. It is only when the fires in the individual heart, or that of a denomination, are dying down that convention frowns on exuberance. The first Christians were accused of being drunk. The first Franciscans had to be reproved for laughing in church. The first Methodists took some of their hymn tunes from the world and set the songs of Zion to dance music. Devotion and exuberance can belong together. We probably don't see as much of it as we should.

FURTHER STUDY

2 Sam. 6:1–23;
Psa. 47:1–9; 150:1–6

1. If exuberance seems irreverent, consider the implications of 2 Samuel 6.

2. What is the justification for exuberant worship?

⊷ *Prayer* ⊷

My Father and my God, You do not withhold Yourself from me, and when I do not withhold myself from You, joy and exuberance are inevitable. If my temperament hinders me from shouting "Hallelujah," then help me to at least whisper it. Amen.

How to sustain joy

"... all Israel contributed the daily portions for the singers and gatekeepers." (v.47)

For reading & meditation – Nehemiah 12:44–47

*I*t is easy to join with others in a time of great rejoicing and sing (and even dance), but true praise is not momentary; rather, it involves honoring God continually.

The phrase "At that time" (v.44) suggests that during the period of renewed inspiration and impetus the people of Judah take steps to ensure that those who serve God by working in the Temple will be well cared for. Their concern is not only for the priests but for those who minister alongside them also – the singers and the gatekeepers. They are now aware that if they are careless and indolent regarding the ministry in the Temple they will suffer the consequences of such neglect. The words "all Israel contributed" show us what an impact recent events have had, for the people are united in their efforts to do everything necessary to provide for those ministering in the Temple. It is interesting to note too that this is the first and only time the term "Israel" appears in this section. Previously attention had been drawn to the sons of Benjamin and the sons of Judah, but now the focus is on "Israel." The parts are now swallowed up in the whole.

The teaching of this passage is not without significance for us today. When we are right with God, other things quickly fall into place. We forget our tribalism (denominations) and think more in terms of the Church. We delight to minister to those who minister to us in Christ's Name and give God's Word its rightful place. Joy can never be sustained apart from that.

FURTHER STUDY

**Psa. 84:1–12;
2 Cor. 9:6–15**

1. What was the real reward for the Temple doorkeepers?

2. What is the outcome of generous giving?

⊷ Prayer ⊷

O God, how I long for this too – that Your Church will be so one with You that everything will fall into its proper place. You may not want to take us out of our denominations but You do want to take the denominations out of us. Help us, dear Father. Amen.

Opening up the Word

"On that day the Book of Moses was read aloud in the hearing of the people ..." (v.1)

For reading & meditation – Nehemiah 13:1–3

One commentator has pointed out that if Nehemiah's memoirs had been an historical novel instead of an accurate portrayal of events, then bringing down the curtain at the end of chapter 12 would have concluded the story perfectly. Instead, however, there is a sad sequel. This proves the wisdom of Thomas Jefferson's observation: "Eternal vigilance is the price of freedom."

Nehemiah was initially governor of Jerusalem for a period of twelve years (445–433 BC), after which he returned to the Persian court for a while to serve King Artaxerxes (13:6). Thus we do not know the precise time when the events described in today's section actually took place. Most commentators think they occurred after Nehemiah's first term of office, while he was away from the city. What we do know is that on a certain day the public reading of Scripture reminded the Jews of their special relationship with God as His chosen people. The passage read was undoubtedly Deuteronomy 23:3–6 which states categorically that no Ammonite or Moabite or any of their descendants may become part of the Lord's people. This did not mean that the Ammonites or Moabites could not become converts to Judaism (Ruth the Moabitess being an example of this), but those who did not embrace the faith had to be excluded from any and all of Israel's activities.

Once again we notice how the public reading of the Scriptures convicted the Jewish people of their obligations and responsibilities as God's people. We can never tell what will happen when we open up our Bibles. But the more we do so, the more good things are likely to happen.

FURTHER STUDY

Luke 4:14–30;
Acts 2:14–41

1. What 1 element in Jesus' sermon resulted in Him being rejected?

2. What 2 elements in Peter's sermon resulted in 3,000 conversions?

⊹ *Prayer* ⊹

Father, once more I am reminded of the need to expose myself to Your Word on a regular basis. Show me even more clearly that whatever else I neglect in my life, I dare not neglect that. In Christ's Name I ask it. Amen.

An intruder in God's house

"Remember me for this, O my God, and do not blot out what I have so faithfully done ..." (v.14)

For reading & meditation – Nehemiah 13:4–14

*I*t is clear in chapter 13 that Nehemiah has been away from Jerusalem some time (v.6), and during his absence things have begun to deteriorate. On returning to the city he makes the astonishing discovery that Eliashib the high priest has turned a large room in the Temple into a home for Tobiah, who was one of Nehemiah's chief enemies. When Nehemiah learns about this he takes it upon himself to go to the Temple, throws Tobiah's furniture out into the street and then orders the rooms to be purified and refurnished with the things that belonged to the house of God. Significantly, Eliashib does nothing to deter him. He realizes that in Nehemiah he has met his match.

The presence of Tobiah in God's house and the negligence of the officials clearly had a bad effect on the people as they were no longer providing for the work of the Temple. Thus the Levites, unable to support their families, had to go back to toiling in their fields. Nehemiah is deeply incensed with all this and, after rebuking the officials, sets about correcting the wrongs. He puts Shelemiah the priest, Zadok the scribe and a Levite named Pedaiah in charge of the Temple storerooms, assisted by Hanan, because "these men were considered trustworthy" (v.13). The backslidden Eliashib disappears from the scene.

How desperately we need men like Nehemiah in today's Church. For too long we have courted the favor of God's enemies. There are people who need rebuking and trends that need challenging. Something drastic has to happen in God's house when the devil lives in the vestry!

FURTHER STUDY

Mark 11:15–17;
3 John vv. 9–11;
Jude vv. 1–25

1. What was the cause of Diotrephes's difficult behavior?

2. What advice does Jude give regarding intrusions into the Church?

⤙⤙ *Prayer* ⤚⤚

O God, protect Your people from the dangers of compromise I pray, and purify us so that Satan will not be able to find a lodging place in our midst. This we ask in our Lord's peerless and precious Name. Amen.

A desecrated Sabbath

"From that time on they no longer came on the Sabbath." (v.21)

For reading & meditation – Nehemiah 13:15–22

Having taken care of the primary cause of the spiritual decline in Jerusalem – compromise in the house of God – Nehemiah now sets about rectifying another major abuse: the desecration of the Sabbath. As he makes his way around the city and the outlying areas he sees Jews treading winepresses on the Sabbath, and others bringing sacks of grain and other produce to Jerusalem in readiness for market the next day. In one instance he sees men from Tyre actually holding an open market on Israel's holy day. Nehemiah once again goes straight to the heart of the issue and proceeds to challenge the leaders with these blunt and outspoken words: "What is this wicked thing you are doing?" (v.17). In case the nobles responsible remain indifferent, Nehemiah steps in and commands the city gates to be closed before the Sabbath so that no merchandise can be brought into Jerusalem. On one or two occasions the merchants and sellers spend a night outside Jerusalem, and appear to have defiantly plied their trade there. Consequently Nehemiah threatens them with imprisonment – a threat they appear to take seriously for they refrain from doing so again.

Living as we do in a secular society, it is seemingly impossible to convince our leaders of the benefits of keeping the Sabbath. But we must keep on trying nevertheless. The moral decline we see is not due entirely to the desecration of the Sabbath, of course, but there is no doubt in my mind that it has something to do with it. As we said earlier – we either take God's commandments or take the consequences.

FURTHER STUDY

Ex. 20:8–11;
Luke 6:1–11; 13:10–17

1. Why should the Sabbath day be kept holy?

2. What did Jesus teach about observing the Sabbath?

⊷ *Prayer* ⊶

O Father, though the world is becoming insensitive to spiritual values and realities, let this situation never develop in Your Church. Wake us up, Lord. Shake us if necessary. In Jesus' Name we ask it. Amen.

The final scenes

"Remember me with favor, O my God." (v.31)

For reading & meditation – Nehemiah 13:23–31

Nehemiah's final reform concerns mixed marriages. He discovers that Jews have intermarried with women from Ashdod, Ammon and Moab. It's the old story – forbidden things have more appeal than those given for our good. When Nehemiah discovers this flagrant violation of the covenant they had made, he becomes so angry that he departs from the principles for handling anger which we saw him practice earlier and strikes some of the men responsible – at the same time pulling out their hair! He discovers also that the grandson of Eliashib the high priest has married the daughter of Sanballat, and his response to this is to drive him away. The enthusiastic Nehemiah (sometimes slightly over-enthusiastic) soon completes his reforms and once again the people settle down to a period of peace and spiritual distinctiveness. Four times in this chapter his prayers begin with the word "Remember." Some think it was because he was discouraged. I prefer to think it was because he lived his entire life in the presence of God and was always ready to lift his heart in prayer to Him.

How do we summarize what we learn from the life of this great and godly man? Without strong and capable spiritual leadership the people of God are like sheep without a shepherd. Moral and spiritual decline then soon sets in. To counteract this we must return to the Word of God, submit ourselves to it, confess our failures and our shortcomings and begin once again to delight in obeying the commandments of the Lord. Only then can we expect to be a people who reflect the glory of the Lord.

FURTHER STUDY

Matt. 9:35–38;
2 Tim. 3:14–17; 4:1–5

1. How did Jesus respond to those without a shepherd?

2. Why should we continue in what we have learned?

⇢ *Prayer* ⇠

O God, may this be not an end but a beginning. Give me the same burden that You gave Nehemiah – the burden to see broken-down walls rebuilt, and Your honor fully restored in the midst of Your people. In Jesus' Name. Amen.

SECTION THREE

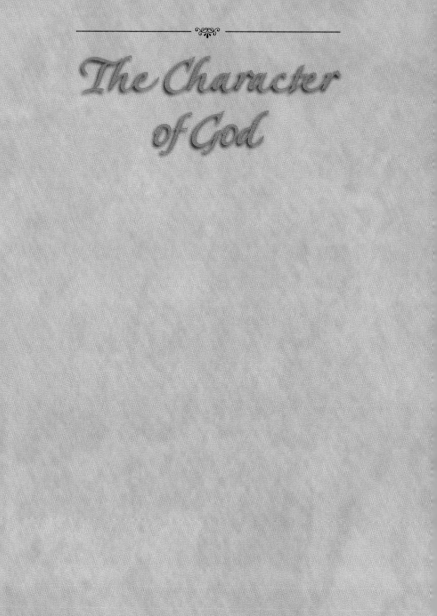

The Character
of God

The Character of God

――――――― ❧ ―――――――

*E*very artist has his own way of representing invisible things in his work. Thomas Kinkade can see a mountain or a child's smile and attempt to capture it with paint and brush. But he can't actually see hope or sadness or honesty. These are abstract characteristics that he can only show indirectly by depicting their results. Though God is invisible, we see His character by looking at His accomplishments and the evidence of His presence. We see God in the way He works at the center of our spiritual lives.

A painting always has a focal point, a reference that gives a visual context to everything else. Certainly in issues of faith, the character of God must be our spiritual focal point. We tend to be interested in selfish and subjective topics; the character of God reclaims our attention. While witnessing to others, church growth, theological issues and all the rest are important, we can understand them only in the context of their relationship to the character of God. We must put His glory above all else; otherwise there's no other question worth asking.

In this section of *Every Day Light*, Selwyn hosts a treasure hunt from one end of the Bible to the other, uncovering gems of guidance and commentary on the character of God – what it is, how we can know it, and how it shapes our world. In Deuteronomy, Isaiah, Psalms, Proverbs, 1 John, and many other books in between, he alights on one verse after another that shapes an image for us of our great Creator and Redeemer; then he interprets them with a skill and insight that are a blessing to all who read his work.

We discover that God reveals His character by healing hearts that are hopelessly broken; by raising up great men to do His work; by guiding the world in fulfillment of His perfect will; by calling vengeance down on those who would oppose Him; by saving sinners incapable of saving themselves.

Most miraculous of all, God chose to make us in His image. The better we understand Him, the better we will know ourselves.

L.G.G.

The primary focus

"In the beginning God ..." (v.1)
For reading & meditation – Genesis 1:1–12

*W*e focus on what without doubt is the most noble and loftiest of themes – *the nature and character of God*. I have noticed that Christians, generally speaking, seem to be preoccupied with knowing more about themselves rather than knowing more about God. Ask any Christian bookshop manager: "What are the best-selling books?" Not those that unfold for us the nature of God, but those that direct us toward such things as how to get a better self-image, how to manage money, how to find inner healing, how to get more excitement out of life, and so on. Not that these subjects are unimportant, but they are explored in a self-absorbed way that gives the idea that the most important thing in life is knowing ourselves better. It isn't. The most important thing in life is knowing God better.

John Lancaster, a minister in Cardiff, South Wales, in an article entitled "Where on earth is God?" asks the question: "Given a choice between attending a seminar, say, on the 'Glory of God in Isaiah' and one on 'The Christian and Sex,' to which would you go?" He makes the point also that though the Church often answers the questions that people are asking, the real problem may be that people are not asking the right questions. In today's Church we are far too man-centered, and not God-centered. It is not by accident, I believe, that the Bible opens with the thunderous acclaim: "In the beginning God ..." I tell you with all the conviction of which I am capable – if God is not our primary focus, then everything else will soon get out of focus.

FURTHER STUDY

John 1:1–5;
Col. 1:15–20;
Heb. 12:2;
Rev. 1:8

1. What did the Lord declare to John the revelator?

2. What did the apostle John declare?

⁂ *Prayer* ⁂

O Father, from this day help me determine to make You my primary focus. And give me the grace and strength to maintain it, through all the vicissitudes and uncertainties of the days ahead. In Jesus' Name I pray. Amen.

A lost art

"Who has known the mind of the Lord?
Or who has been his counselor?" (v.34)

For reading & meditation – Romans 11:25–36

A subject which is of great interest to many today is anthropology – the study of man. Although this subject is of great importance, for a Christian there is something far more important – the study of God. The great preacher C. H. Spurgeon said: "The highest science, the loftiest speculation, the mightiest philosophy that can ever engage the attention of a child of God, is the name, the nature, the person, the work, the doings, and the existence of the great God whom he calls his Father."

The contemplation of God seems to be a lost art today. We appear to be more concerned about subjects such as Church growth, the end times, signs, wonders and miracles. I am not suggesting these issues are unimportant, but they must not be allowed to replace the supremely important matter of the constant, earnest and continued investigation of the great subject of the Deity. The more we know of God the more effective will be our lives here on earth. Those who have given themselves to the study of God tell us that it humbles the mind, expands the soul, and consoles the heart.

It humbles the mind. When our minds grapple with other subjects we feel a degree of self-content and come away thinking: "Behold, I am wise." But when our minds engage with thoughts of God we discover that there is no plumb-line that can sound His depth, and we come away thinking: "Behold, I know nothing." In an age which stresses the supremacy of the human ego it is no bad thing to learn that there is something far greater. Indeed *someone* far greater – the infinite and eternal God.

FURTHER STUDY

Isa. 40:18–26;
Job 11:7–9

1. What probing question does Isaiah ask?

2. What conclusion had Zophar come to?

Prayer

Gracious and loving heavenly Father, teach me how to focus on You and contemplate You so that all vanity and pride dies within me, and I go on my way no longer caught up with how wise I am but how wonderful You are. In Jesus' Name. Amen.

Quiet contemplation

"For you make me glad by your deeds, O Lord ..." (v.4)
For reading & meditation – Psalm 92:1–15

How does contemplation of God expand the soul? "The soul," says one theologian, "is at home only when it is in God." He meant, of course, that as the soul was made for God it can only function effectively when indwelt by God. Contemplation of God is like breath to the soul; it inflates it and causes it to be fully actualized. "My body and my whole physiology functions better when God is in it," said a doctor to me some years ago. I replied: "And so it is also with the soul, dear Doctor, so it is also with the soul."

The third benefit of contemplating God is that it consoles the heart. But how? It does so by focusing the heart's attention on the greatness and goodness of the Eternal and also on His tender mercies and compassion. The more we know of God the more we will realize that when He permits us to pass through deep and dark waters it is not because He is powerless to deliver us, but because a beneficent and eternal purpose is being worked out in that process. And what is more, we discover that God is not interested merely in working out His purposes in us, but imparting to us a richer sense of His presence. In God there is a balm for every wound, a comfort for every sorrow, and healing for every heartache. All kinds of nostrums are on offer in today's Church to help those who are hurting (some of them more secular than sacred), but I know of nothing that calms the swelling billows of sorrow and grief as does the quiet contemplation of the Godhead.

FURTHER STUDY

Psa. 145:1–21;
Deut. 32:1–4;
1 Chron. 29:10–13

1. How did David express the feelings of his soul?

2. How did Moses put it?

✦ *Prayer* ✦

My Father and my God, forgive me if in times of trial and distress I look for comfort in the wrong places. You and You alone are able to meet my soul's deepest needs. Help me see that not merely as an opinion but as a conviction. In Jesus' Name. Amen.

"Eccentric" Christians

*"He sits enthroned above the circle of the earth,
and its people are like grasshoppers." (v.22)*

For reading & meditation – Isaiah 40:21–31

The man-centered focus that is creeping into today's Church must be resisted at all costs. Such matters as disciplining children, marital problems and establishing proper priorities should be addressed also, but we must be careful that "market forces" do not mold our theology. People may *want* to know about these issues, but what they *need*, primarily, is to know God.

It could be argued that our problems are so acute because we are deficient in our knowledge of God. The context in which we think and feel is so limited that it is no wonder our souls feel stifled and claustrophobic. One preacher describes our condition in this way: "We are like Peter trying to walk on the water but becoming so engrossed in the winds and the waves that we lose sight of the all-sufficient Christ who is right there beside us. The immediate environment has blotted out the sense of the eternal."

This is why I have chosen today's reading from the magnificent book of Isaiah. The prophet does what a doctor would do upon visiting a patient with a minor sickness and finding the windows shut fast and the room lacking in oxygen. He would throw open the windows and invite the patient to inhale the purer air. "Take a deep breath of the oxygen of the Spirit," Isaiah is saying in effect. "See how great and powerful God is. Set your problems in the context of His might and omnipotence." We become like the thing we focus on. If we center on man rather than God then we ought not be surprised if we finish up off center – eccentric.

FURTHER STUDY

2 Cor. 4:13–18;
Heb. 3:1; 12:2;
Psa. 141:8

1. What was Paul's focus?

2. What is the exhortation of the writer of Hebrews?

✦—✦ *Prayer* ✦—✦

O God, save me from being an off-center Christian and thus an eccentric Christian – the true meaning of that term. May my primary focus be always on You. Grant it, dear Lord. In Jesus' Name I pray. Amen.

Stirred - but not shaken

"Because he is at my right hand, I shall not be shaken." (v.8)
For reading & meditation – Psalm 16:1–11

We continue expanding the theme we touched on yesterday – the danger of allowing our faith to become more man-centered than God-centered. Whenever I have the opportunity to address Christian counselors I try to urge them to put the glory of God before their client's well-being. A good deal of "Christian counseling" today follows the client-centerd approach where the person is all-important. Thus more attention is paid to how the person has been hurt by others than how he or she may be hurting God by being unwilling to trust Him. This is a very sensitive issue, and I tell counselors in training that it must *never* be brought up until other issues have been explored and understood. But ultimately, however, this is the issue we must all face, whether we are in counseling or not.

Ask yourself this question now: Do I allow myself to be more overwhelmed by the wrong people have done to me than the wrong I might have done (and may still be doing) to God by my unwillingness to trust Him? Putting the glory of God before our well-being does not go down well with some modern-day Christians brought up in the "Me" generation. It means that we have to break away from the idea that life revolves around our desires, our ambitions, our self-image, our personal comfort, our hurts and problems, but instead around the glory and the will of God. When we learn to apply the great text before us today to our lives we will find, as did the psalmist, that when we set the Lord always before us then no matter what happens we will be stirred, but not shaken.

FURTHER STUDY

1 Sam. 4:1–22;
Ex. 33:12–18;
Psa. 29:1–2

1. Is there a parallel between this account and today's Church?

2. What was Moses' request?

⊶ *Prayer* ⊷

Father, thank You for reminding me that I cannot avoid my soul being "stirred" by life's problems, but when I have set You ever before me, then I can avoid being "shaken." Drive this truth deep into my being this very day. In Jesus' Name. Amen.

God marginalized

"... but let him who boasts boast about this: that he understands and knows me ..." (v.24)

For reading & meditation – Jeremiah 9:17–24

A minister speaking at a recent conference of a well-known denomination said: "The reason why there is so much depletion of spiritual energy in people nowadays is due to the rush of modern-day life." But is this really true? If it is then it puts the blame for our condition outside of us rather than inside us – the place (in my opinion) where the fault really lies. No, the real reason for the spiritual dullness in so many lives is that we have lost our sense of priority. One of my favorite poets is Wordsworth, and I simply love the lines that go thus:

The world is too much with us; late and soon
Getting and spending we lay waste our powers;
Little we see in Nature that is ours;
We have given our hearts away ...

The world is too much with us! Therein lies our problem. Other things, other issues, other problems, other priorities have been allowed to press in upon us, and the consequence of all this is that God has become marginalized. If we were to pay as much attention to the things that pertain to God as we do to the things that pertain to the world then the spiritual health of the Church (generally speaking) would not be such a cause for concern.

Through the prophet Jeremiah God speaks to us and shows us that His greatest desire is that we should come to know Him. When we lose God we lose touch with reality, for reality, as one great Christian put it, is Jesus' other Name.

FURTHER STUDY

Jer. 2:1–13; 17:13;
Isa. 53:6

1. What 2 sins had Israel committed?

2. What broken cisterns does the Church drink at?

✦ *Prayer* ✦

O God, forgive me that so often my desires are at cross-purposes with Your desires. My desire is to know more about me; Your desire is for me to know more about You. Help me bring my desires in line with Your desires. In Jesus' Name. Amen.

"Nutty" – the right word

"Your love is like the morning mist, like the early dew that disappears." (v.4)

For reading & meditation – Hosea 6:1–11

A danger that we must acquaint ourselves with as we discuss the need to contemplate God more deeply is that of becoming more interested in godliness than in God Himself. Theologian Jim Packer puts the point effectively when he says that "moving in evangelical circles as I do I am often troubled by what I find. While my fellow believers are constantly seeking to advance in godliness, they show little direct interest in God Himself. When they study Scripture, only the principles of personal godliness get their attention; their heavenly Father does not. It is as if they should concentrate on the ethics of marriage and fail to spend time with their spouse!" He goes on to say: "There is something narcissistic, and, to tell the truth, nutty in being more concerned with godliness than about God." I think "nutty" is the right word.

I knew a man who went to every seminar he could find on the subject of marriage, and whenever he came upon a new idea of a deep insight he would reflect for hours on its wonder and profundity. The only trouble was he never got past the reflecting stage, and while he indulged himself in new and profound ideas, his wife was left languishing at home.

How sad that a man can take more interest in the principles that undergird his marriage than in the partner whom he has pledged to love, honor, and cherish. Let's be watchful that we don't care more for the principles of godliness than the God we are called to praise and please every day of our lives.

FURTHER STUDY

2 Tim. 3:1–5;
2 Chron. 25:1–2;
Isa. 29:13

1. What is one of the signs of the last days?

2. What is said of Amaziah?

✦ *Prayer* ✦

Gracious and loving heavenly Father, forgive me I pray if I have been caught up more in the mechanics of my faith than in the dynamics of it. May nothing ever become more important to me than my relationship with You. Amen.

Seeing the invisible

"... he persevered because he saw him who is invisible." (v.27)

For reading & meditation – Hebrews 11:17–28

hat is it that prompts some people to take more interest in the principles of godliness than in God Himself? I think one reason could be that we are more comfortable dealing in the realm of the visible than the invisible. We prefer to work with things we can touch or handle and apply so that we feel an immediate impact rather than to launch out into the unseen and simply trust.

I often saw people come up against this problem in the days when much of my time was spent in personal counselling. I would bring people to a place where they could accept that the roots of their problem lay in a deficient relationship with God. However, when a movement toward Him of simple basic trust was called for, terror would appear for a moment in their eyes and they would say: "Give me some steps I can take to deal with my problem, some principles I can follow that will act as a ladder on which I can climb out of this pit."

We all find it easier to *do* than to *be*; we prefer a plan to follow rather than a Person to trust. What our carnal nature hates to be faced with is the challenge of throwing ourselves in utter dependency on a God who is invisible and intangible. Yet this is what a relationship with God entails. The thing that marks Moses out as outstanding in the chapter before us today is not his works but his faith. He persevered because he saw Him who is *invisible*. It is possible to see the invisible, but it is possible only to the eye of faith.

FURTHER STUDY

Rom. 1:16–23;
Heb. 11:1–2;
1 Tim. 1:17

1. Why are men without excuse?
2. What is the essence of faith?

➻ *Prayer* ↢

My Father and my God, help me recognize this terrible tendency in myself to be more comfortable with working than trusting. Let Your Word reach deep into my heart today. Teach me how to be. In Jesus' Name I pray. Amen.

Balanced Christianity

"After beginning with the Spirit, are you now trying to attain your goal by human effort?" (v.3)

For reading & meditation – Galatians 3:1-25

The Christian Church has always struggled to get the balance right between faith and works. Romans is the great book on "faith" while James is the great book on "works." I know some Christians who never read the book of James, taking sides with Martin Luther who called it a "book of straw." Martin Luther may have been right about many things but he was wrong when he referred to the Epistle of James in this way. We need to study both Romans and James if we want to be properly balanced Christians.

The difficulty with faith and works is this: we come into the Christian life by depending on the innocent sufferings of our Lord Jesus Christ on Calvary as sufficient ground for our acceptance with God, and then when we learn the principles of Christian living we turn from dependency on Christ to dependency on them. This was the great problem in the Galatian churches and it is still a problem here in the Church of the twentieth century. Bringing forth the fruit of repentance by good works is terribly important but we are not to *depend* on works for our salvation.

We tend to focus more on works than faith because it is something visible and tangible. We can see what we are doing and assess it or measure it. Faith is different. It requires of us a degree of helplessness (something the carnal nature detests), but if we are to know God better and avoid falling into the trap of pursuing godliness more keenly than God, then faith must be seen as the primary virtue.

FURTHER STUDY

Eph. 2:1–9;
Gal. 2:16;
Rom. 9:32

1. What did Paul remind the Ephesians?

2. What did he emphasise to the Galatians?

↦ Prayer ↤

O Father, help me get this right. I am saved to good works but I am not saved by good works. Prevent me from falling into the trap of being more preoccupied with Your principles than with You Yourself. In Jesus' Name. Amen.

Meeting the Person

"I want to know Christ and the power of his resurrection ..." (v.10)

For reading & meditation – Philippians 3:1–14

W̲e spend one more day setting the stage before lifting the curtains on this most important subject of the nature and character of God. It must not be assumed from what has been said over the past couple of days that the study of Scripture and contemplation of the principles which God has built into His Word are unimportant. They most certainly are. What I am saying is this – let us be on our guard that we do not fall into the trap of contemplating the principles which God has built into the universe more than God Himself.

I have often seen students of Scripture fall into this trap when, in reading their Bible, the only things that get their attention are the principles that relate to godliness. They underline them in their Bible, mark alongside them other Scriptural references, and think that by doing this they are growing spiritually. The problem, however, is that only the principles of daily personal godliness capture their interest; their heavenly Father does not.

FURTHER STUDY

Rev. 2:1–7;
2 Cor. 5:14

1. What was the church in Ephesus commended for?

2. Why was this insufficient?

Imagine treating a love letter that way: identifying and underlining the principles, reflecting on the profundity of some of the insights, marvelling at the clarity of the language and yet missing the main purpose of the letter – romantic passion and love. Yet this is the way some people approach the Bible. Our aim in studying the nature and character of God must be to know God better (not merely know His Word better), and we must seek to enlarge our acquaintance not simply with the characteristics of His nature, but with the living God whose characteristics they are.

⊷ *Prayer* ⊶

O God, help me never to approach the Bible content to know only the written Word. Give me a passion that never remains satisfied until, through the written Word, I discover more of the living Word. In Jesus' Name. Amen.

God's self-revelation

*"But those who trust in idols ... will be turned back
in utter shame." (v.17)*

For reading & meditation – Isaiah 42:10–17

*W*e are ready now to close in on our subject and contemplate as far as we are able the nature and character of the God we worship. Most of what we know about God is from His self-revelation in the Scriptures. We know something about Him as we look out through the lattice of nature, but because the world of nature has been affected by the Fall we cannot expect to find a clear revelation of Him there. Scripture, however, is different. The Bible (I believe) has been supernaturally protected from the effects and influences of sin, and in its pages we have a clear revelation of who God is and what He is like. This is why all human ideas about God, His will and His work, both traditional and contemporary, must be ruthlessly brought in line with what Scripture says.

Those who think they can get a clear picture of God apart from Scripture are misguided and deceived. A young Christian once said to me: "I don't need to read the Bible to know God; I simply sit and meditate on Him and He reveals Himself to me." He thought he could know God in this way but he was mistaken. When we try to know God or understand Him through the medium of our own conceptions, then our conceptions are the medium.

The Bible is God's revelation of Himself, and unless our thoughts are guided and constantly corrected by God's thoughts we will soon go off on tangents. We need to remember that idolatry – which really is forming unbiblical notions of God and thus worshipping unrealities – is the sin that is most frequently denounced in Scripture.

FURTHER STUDY

Ex. 20:1–7;
Deut. 11:16;
1 John 5:21

1. What were the children of Israel to be careful about?

2. What was John's admonition to the Church?

↦ *Prayer* ↤

O God, help me understand more than ever that it is the entrance of Your Word that gives light, and the neglecting of Your Word that gives darkness. May I take Your light as my light, and thus walk through life with a sure and steady tread. Amen.

The great Creator

"... he who created the heavens and stretched them out,
who spread out the earth ..." (v.5)

For reading & meditation – Isaiah 42:1–9

*W*hat is the first thing we learn about God as we open up the Scriptures? It is His might and omnipotence. The Bible never argues that there is a God; everywhere it assumes and asserts the fact. Majestically the opening verse of Scripture says: "In the beginning God ..." Its paramount concern is not to persuade us that God *is*, but to tell us who God is and what He *does*. The first thing we see Him do in the Scriptures is to act creatively.

I love the story concerning a group of researchers who set out to discover what really happened when the earth was created. They spent months gathering information and feeding data into a computer. Finally they hit the printout key and waited. Soon a message appeared with these words: "See Genesis 1:1."

Many think the only reference to God's creative act is the one which appears in the first two chapters of Genesis, but the truth is woven inextricably into the very texture of both the Old and the New Testament. One example of this is found in our text for today.

FURTHER STUDY

Acts 14:8–15;
Neh. 9:5–6;
Psa. 102:25;
Heb. 11:3

1. What did Paul and Barnabas declare?

2. How do we understand that God formed the universe?

We cannot have a right conception of God or contemplate Him correctly unless we think of Him as all-powerful. He who cannot do what He wills and pleases cannot be God. As God has a will to do good, so He has the necessary power to execute that will. Who can look upward to the midnight sky, behold its wonders and not exclaim: "Of what were these mighty orbs formed?" A great and powerful God brought them into being simply by saying: "Let them be." This kind of God can have my heart anytime.

⟶ *Prayer* ⟵

Father, I sense that the more enlightened my understanding the more my soul responds to that enlightenment with thanksgiving, adoration, and praise. Enlighten me still more, dear Father. In Jesus' Name I pray. Amen.

"Not from me!"

"By the word of the Lord were the heavens made, their starry host by the breath of his mouth." (v.6)

For reading & meditation – Psalm 33:1–22

oday, the idea that God created the world is scoffed at by many. Modern astronomers probing into outer space with their gigantic telescopes favor two theories as to the origin of the universe. One is the so-called Big Bang Theory, according to which "The cosmos started with a titanic explosion and as a consequence has been expanding ever since." The other is the Continuous Creation Theory which maintains that "The universe is self-creating and is constantly making itself out of nothing and falling back into nothingness again."

What many scientists are not prepared to admit is that the ultimate energy behind the universe is a not a Big Bang, but a Big Being – an intelligent Being of indescribable majesty and power who is able to do whatever He chooses. And because what He chooses is always good, He can be trusted to have the best interest of His creation at heart. When Joseph Haydn, the famous Austrian composer, had finished his great oratorio *The Creation*, he is said to have cried: "Not from me! Not from me! From above it has all come!"

Our text for today reminds us that by God's Word were the heavens made and by His breath the stars were formed. I once heard my father, a local preacher, picturesquely describe the creation in this way: "It was no harder for God to create a world than it is for my son to blow soap bubbles into the air out of his clay pipe." I go back to that lovely image often nowadays. I find that when contemplating this awesome, mighty, all-powerful God, my soul instinctively cries: "How great Thou art." I hope yours does too!

FURTHER STUDY

Matt. 19:16–26;
1 Chron. 29:12;
Psa. 62:11;
Isa. 43:12–13

1. What did Jesus declare?

2. What did God declare?

⊷ *Prayer* ⊷

Yes Father, as I contemplate Your majesty and Your power my soul cries out also: "How great Thou art." It can do nothing else, for contemplation of You inevitably leads to adoration of You. Amen.

Sustained and secure

"These all look to you to give them their food at the proper time."
(v.27)

For reading & meditation – Psalm 104:1–35

Now we consider God's might and power in the act of preservation. No creature has power to preserve itself. "Can papyrus grow tall where there is no marsh?" asked Job (Job 8:11). Both man and beast would perish if there were no food, and there would be no food if the earth were not refreshed with fruitful showers. As one preacher put it: "We came from God's hand and we remain in His hand."

Think of the marvel of life in the womb. How an infant can live for so many months in such a cramped environment – and without breathing – is unaccountable except for the power of God in preservation. It was divine preservation Daniel was thinking of when he said to the godless Belshazzar: "You did not honor the God who holds in his hand your life and all your ways" (Dan. 5:23). Everywhere in the Scriptures God is presented not only as the Creator of the world but as its Sustainer and Preserver also.

God has not wound up the universe like a clock and then separated Himself from it; He is active in sustaining it, and were He to remove Himself from it, it would cease to exist. The writer to the Hebrews reminds us that He is *"upholding* all things by the word of his power"* (1:3, KJV). If the maker of some artifact were to die, his death would make no difference to it. It would continue to exist just as it did before. Not so with God and His world, however. If God were to die the universe would fall to pieces. But don't worry – God cannot die. The universe is quite secure.

FURTHER STUDY

Isa. 46:1–13;
Psa. 18:35; 147:6

1. What did the Lord underline to the children of Israel?

2. What did the psalmist testify?

⊶ Prayer ⊷

O God, when I consider how You are my Sustainer and my Preserver my heart is humbled before You. You cannot die and because I am linked to You, I cannot die. I know my body will die but my soul is Yours – forever. Thank You dear Father. Amen.

This God is your God

*"Will your courage endure or your hands be strong
in the day I deal with you?" (v.14)*

For reading & meditation – Ezekiel 22:1–16

God is powerful in *judgment*. When He smites none can resist Him, as our text for today so clearly shows. The Flood of Noah's day is one such example, when the entire race – with the exception of eight people – was swept away (Gen. 6:1–9:18). A shower of fire and brimstone from heaven and Sodom and Gomorrah and all the cities of the plain were destroyed (Gen. 19:1–29). Pharaoh and his hosts were impotent when God blew upon them at the Red Sea (Ex. 14:1–31).

What does the contemplation of God's great power do for us? First, it causes us to *tremble* before Him. The trouble with many modern men and women is that they do not *tremble* before God. To treat with impudence the One who can crush us more easily than we can an ant is, as someone put it, "a suicidal policy." "Kiss the Son," said the psalmist, "lest he be angry and you be destroyed ... for his wrath can flare up in a moment" (Psa. 2:12).

Second, contemplating God's great power causes us to *adore* Him. Who can consider the might of this awesome God without wanting to worship Him? The rebellious heart will resist this, but the heart cleansed by the blood of Christ will bow in homage and say: "Who is like you – majestic in holiness, awesome in glory, working wonders?" (Ex. 15:11).

Well may we as believers *trust* such a God. No prayer is too hard for Him to answer, no need too great for Him to supply, no predicament too great for Him to solve. Lay hold on this great and gripping truth: this God is *your* God.

FURTHER STUDY

Psa. 114:1–8;
1 Chron. 16:30–31;
Isa. 66:1–3

1. What can the presence
of the
Lord do?

2. Who does the
Lord esteem?

✦ *Prayer* ✦

O Father, I see that contemplation of You tilts my soul in Your direction. I realize that without You I am nothing. May I tremble before You until my trembling turns to adoration and ever-increasing trust. Amen.

The God who speaks

"... so are my ways higher than your ways and my thoughts than your thoughts." (v.9)

For reading & meditation – Isaiah 55:1–13

After seeing in Genesis 1 that God is all-powerful, the next thing we observe about God is that He is *personal.* But what does it mean to be a person? What predicates personality? The best definition of personality I know is the one given to me by the tutor who taught me theology: "To be a person we have to be able to think, to reason, to feel, to judge, to choose and to communicate in words that constitute a language." Richard Swinburne, a theologian, observes that people use language not only to communicate and for private thought, but to argue, to raise a consideration, to object to another. Unlike animals which show evidence only of wanting food and drink, people can want *not* to want something, like a fasting man, for example, wanting not to want food.

Now with that in mind – that one of the constituents of personality is the ability to think and speak – read the first chapter of Genesis once again. Notice how many times the words appear: "God said." Count them. God is portrayed to us as a *speaking* God, and speech being one of the constituent parts of personality this proves that the Deity is a *personal* Being. We are not long into Genesis before we are brought face to face with the fact that there is more to God than mere power; the Almighty is a Person. This means, among other things, that the Almighty cannot be studied from a "safe" distance. Because He is a Person He is someone who wants and waits to be "known."

FURTHER STUDY

Gen. 1:1–31;
Job 33:13–14;
1 Kings 19:12;
Ezek. 43:2

1. How many times does it say "God said"?

2. How did Ezekiel describe God's voice?

✦ *Prayer* ✦

Loving heavenly Father, how thankful I am that You made me like Yourself – to know and be known. May my strongest desire be to know You, not merely to know myself. For it is only when I know You that I can most truly know myself. Amen.

"Plenty of time for you"

"How precious to me are your thoughts, O God!
How vast is the sum of them!" (v.17)

For reading & meditation – Psalm 139:1–24

We continue exploring the fact that God is not only powerful, but personal. The constituent parts of personality are predicated of God on almost every page of the Bible. "I will raise up for myself a faithful priest, who will do according to what is in my heart and mind," said the Lord to Eli in 1 Samuel 2:35. This shows (if it needs showing) that God has a mind with which He thinks.

God has emotions also – another aspect of personality. Some modern-day theologians claim that God is unable to feel, but clearly this is not supported by Scripture. God can be angry (Psa. 2:12), jealous (Zech. 1:14–15), merciful (Psa. 78:38), and joyful (Deut. 30:9). These are just a few of the emotions which Scripture talks about, but there are many more. Again, God *chooses* and *decides*. "And it repented the Lord that he had made man on the earth ... And the Lord said, I will destroy man whom I have created ..." (Gen. 6:6–7, KJV).

While the majority of human beings believe in some kind of God, many view Him as being so great that He cannot possibly take a personal interest in such insignificant creatures as ourselves. Dr. Henry Norris Russell, one of the great astronomers of this century and a Christian, once gave a talk on the vastness of the universe. Afterwards someone asked him this question: "How is it possible for such a great and infinite God to have time for me?" This was his reply: "An infinite God can dispatch the affairs of this universe in the twinkling of an eye, thus giving Him plenty of time for you."

FURTHER STUDY

Heb. 4:12–16;
Psa. 2:12;
Zech. 1:14–15;
Psa. 78:38;
Deut. 30:9

1. Can you think of other scriptures showing God's emotions?

2. What is God able to do through Christ?

✦ *Prayer* ✦

O Father, help me in the midst of every trial and difficulty to drop my anchor in this reassuring and encouraging revelation – no matter what my problem, You always have plenty of time to give to me. I am so deeply, deeply thankful. Amen.

"Jittery theologians"

"But God said ... 'You fool! This very night your life will be demanded from you.' " (v.20)

For reading & meditation – Luke 12:13–21

Why is it that so many in our day and age are attracted to the notion of a God who is impersonal? New Age theories seem to be infiltrating all parts of society in almost every country of the world.

I think there is a very subtle reason why men and women prefer to think of God as a power rather than as a Person. If God is merely a power, or a formless life-force flowing through the universe, there are no demands – one is not challenged to relate to an energy in the same way that one is challenged to relate to a person. Immediately we believe God is a Person the next question we have to face is: How do I relate to Him? It is the idea of meeting a personal God which causes men and women to tremble.

But deep down in every human heart, placed there by the Almighty, is a conviction that a personal God exists. We have all been made in His image and His stamp is upon us whether we like it or not. In reality there are very few atheists; most people believe in some kind of God. Someone has described an atheist as "a theologian with the jitters." A good way of dealing with those jitters is to expunge from the heart the idea that God may be personal and that one might be accountable to Him. Better a life-force or a celestial energy, a power that can be tapped rather than a Person one might some day have to meet. How foolish it all is – settling for short-term comfort but facing eternal loss.

FURTHER STUDY

Gen. 1:26–30; 5:1;
1 Cor. 11:7;
James 3:9;
Eccl. 3:11

1. What are the implications of being created in God's image?

2. What has God set within us?

⇛ *Prayer* ⇚

Father, I am saddened when I realize how so many want to run from You when their best interests lie in running to You. I am glad that I have found You, but I long that others might find You too. Draw many to You this very day, dear Lord. In Jesus' Name. Amen.

The God who is there

"The fool says in his heart, 'There is no God.' " (v.1)

For reading & meditation – Psalm 14:1–7

The idea of a living personal God gives men and women the jitters. They sense deep within that they are accountable to Him but they don't know just what to do about it.

C. S. Lewis put it like this: "The Pantheist's God does nothing, demands nothing. He is there if you wish for Him, like a book on a shelf. He will not pursue you. There is no danger that at any time heaven and earth should feel awe at His glance. But Christ the Creator King is *there*. And His intervening presence is terribly startling to discover." Lewis goes on to compare the shock of discovering that there is a living personal God in the universe to sitting alone in the dark and sensing someone breathing beside you. "It is always shocking," he says, "to meet life where we thought we were alone."

Listen to this paragraph by Lewis which I quote in full as it puts the truth in a way that cannot be equalled: "There comes a moment when the children who have been playing at burglars hush suddenly; was that a *real* footstep in the hall? There comes a moment when people who have been dabbling in religion suddenly draw back. Supposing we really found Him! We never meant it to come to that! Worse still, supposing He has found us? So it is a sort of Rubicon. One goes across, or not. But if one does there is no manner of security against miracles. One may be in for *anything*." No one need worry about getting any shocks when they steadfastly resist believing in a personal God. No shocks, but no salvation either.

FURTHER STUDY

Psa. 10:1–4; 36:1–4;
1 John 2:22

1. What is at the heart of the atheist?

2. How does John describe those who deny Christ?

✦ *Prayer* ✦

Gracious God, how can I ever sufficiently thank You for bringing me to Yourself? The thought of a God who is alive, taking a personal interest in me, is more than I can comprehend. Yet I believe it. With all my heart. Thank You dear Father. Amen.

The Father God

"When you pray, say: 'Father ...' " (v.2)
For reading & meditation – Luke 11:1–13

*S*amuel Shoemaker, the American Episcopalian preacher who was instrumental in forming Alcoholics Anonymous, pointed out that the whole principle of prayer depends on what kind of Being the Creator is. Listen to this statement made to a group of recovering alcoholics: "If He created the universe and gave everything a primeval push, and then retired beyond, where we cannot get in contact with Him, prayer is a vain effort. But if He be a personal God as Christians believe He is, then He will have a concern for the people He made and will want to involve Himself with them in all their affairs." We are not alone in this universe; a *personal* God stands behind all things, waiting, longing that we might enter into a relationship with Him.

We said that one of the reasons why people desire an impersonal God is because that kind of God is easier to live with than one who is personal like themselves. It's rather nice to carry inside our hearts a subjective idea of a God of beauty, truth and goodness. That kind of God demands nothing of us. Better still a formless life-force surging through all of us, a vast power we can tap and use to our advantage. That kind of God is extremely easy to live with. But a God who approaches us at infinite speed – the Hunter, the King, the Lover, the Husband – that is quite another matter. But whether we believe it or not, that is the kind of God He is.

FURTHER STUDY

Gen. 3:1–8;
Ex. 33:14–17;
Isa. 43:2

1. How did God present Himself as a personal Being?

2. What did He promise Moses?

⊷ Prayer ⊷

Gracious and loving God, how thankful I am that You are not just a supernatural energy or a life-force, but a personal Being whom I can address as "Father." Your personality engages with my personality and we are one. In that my joy knows no bounds. Amen.

On this truth we stand

"... Jesus ... saw ... the Spirit descending ... And a voice came from heaven: 'You are my Son ...' " (vv.10–11)

For reading & meditation – Mark 1:1–13

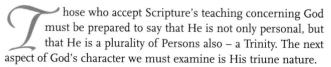

Those who accept Scripture's teaching concerning God must be prepared to say that He is not only personal, but that He is a plurality of Persons also – a Trinity. The next aspect of God's character we must examine is His triune nature.

The doctrine of the Trinity, that God is One yet three separate Persons, is not easy to understand, but it is clear in Scripture. The term "Trinity" nowhere appears in the Bible (it was first used by Tertullian around AD 210), but its roots are deeply embedded in the Word of God. It is mainly a revelation of the New Testament, but there are glimpses of the truth to be seen in the Old Testament also. "Let *us* make man in our image" (Gen. 1:26). To whom was God speaking at this stage? Some say the angels, but nowhere in Scripture are angels seen as being involved in the act of creation or as being on the same level as God. Read Colossians 1:16 and it will become clear to whom God was speaking. "Man has now become like one of *us*" (Gen. 3:22). In Isaiah 6:8 God says: "Whom shall I send? And who will go for *us*?"

"Go to the Jordan," wrote Augustine, "and you find the Trinity. There at the baptism of Jesus the three Persons in the Godhead are simultaneously in evidence. The Father is heard speaking directly from heaven, the Son is seen being immersed in the river, and John the Baptist beholds the Spirit descending upon the Christ." Three in One and One in Three. On this truth we must stand, even though we may not fully understand.

FURTHER STUDY

Matt. 28:16–20
John 14:26–27; 15:26–27

1. How were the disciples to baptize new converts?

2. How did Jesus confirm the truth of the Trinity?

⊷ *Prayer* ⊷

Blessed Trinity, Three in One and One in Three, I worship You this day in spirit and in truth. My spirit joins with Your Spirit, and Your truth, though sometimes darkness to my intellect, is nevertheless sunshine to my heart. Amen.

The baptismal formula

*"... baptizing ... in the name of the Father and of the
Son and of the Holy Spirit ..." (v.19)*

For reading & meditation – Matthew 28:1–20

We ended yesterday with the words of Augustine that if we want to see the Trinity in action then all we have to do is to go to the River Jordan. It was Augustine who pointed out also that the Trinity can be seen in the verse that is before us today, which we call "the baptismal formula." Note that we are bidden to baptize in the Name (not "names") of the Father, Son, and Holy Spirit, indicating their essential unity and oneness.

I know there are many in the Christian Church who do not accept the doctrine of the Trinity and this makes me very sad. I just wish they would look at the matter again, for I have found it to be one of the most satisfying of doctrines as it meets the greatest needs of my soul. George Matheson spoke for me and millions of other Christians when he said:

> *Some seek a Father in the heavens above,*
> *Some ask a human figure to adore,*
> *Some crave a Spirit vast as life and love,*
> *Within thy mansions we have all and more.*

FURTHER STUDY

2 Cor. 13:1–14;
1 Thess. 5:19–24

1. How does Paul affirm the truth of the Trinity?

2. How does he illustrate it?

Alfred Tennyson, a man with an incisive mind who saw deep into the creation, put it like this: "Though nothing is such a distress of soul to me as to hear the divinity of Christ assailed, yet I feel I must never lose the unity of the Godhead, the three persons being like three candles giving together one light." Note his words: "I must never lose the unity of the Godhead." I would simply add: neither must we. Neither must we.

⤙ *Prayer* ⤚

Father, Son and Holy Spirit, I freely confess my mind finds it difficult to comprehend how You can be Three in One, and One in Three. Yet this is the teaching of Scripture. So I believe; help Thou mine unbelief. In Jesus' Name. Amen.

Three great errors

*"I urge you ... by our Lord Jesus Christ and by the love
of the Spirit ... by praying to God ..." (v.30)*

For reading & meditation – Romans 15:23–30

God is One, yet God is Three. How can such a strange thing be?" These are the lines of a ditty that supposedly was sung by troops on the march in World War I. Theologians down the ages have tried to illuminate this doctrine for us, but it is an issue that will never be fully clarified until we arrive in heaven (1 Cor. 13:12). Basically the doctrine of the Trinity is: God is One but with three distinct centers of consciousness.

Around this truth a number of errors have been propounded. The first was the teaching that there are three gods. The Jehovah's Witnesses accuse present-day Christians of believing this, and say that we conceive of God as a body with three heads. That might be true of ancient heresy but it is not true of classic Trinitarianism. The second heresy taught that God is unipersonal and the other two Persons in the Trinity are simply manifestations of the Being of the one God. The third main error denied the equality of the divine Persons and regarded them as being of different rank.

The historic Church formulated the Athanasian Creed which states that we worship one God in Trinity and Trinity in unity. What we must see, however, is that no words can fully explain the truth of the Trinity. "The creed is a safety net to keep us from falling into error," says one preacher, "rather than a verbal net in which to trap the truth." We use the term "Trinity" expecting not so much that in that one word the truth may be spoken, but that it may not be left unspoken.

FURTHER STUDY

1 Pet. 1:1–6;
1 Tim. 2:5

1. How did Peter make a distinction between the members of the Trinity?

2. What did Paul confirm to Timothy?

⊷ *Prayer* ⊷

Father, I see that life often presents me with facts which seem irreconcilable at one stage of knowledge – though better understood at another. Perhaps one day this great mystery of the Trinity may be cleared up. Meanwhile I simply worship and adore. Amen.

Logically necessary

"Give thanks to the God of gods. His love endures forever." (v.2)

For reading & meditation – Psalm 136:1–26

The Trinity is implicit in the whole Bible from the beginning, though it might not be evident to someone unfamiliar with the Book who started reading at Genesis until they had reached the books of the New Testament.

Ian Macpherson, in his book *The Faith Once Delivered*, says that when the island now known as Trinidad was discovered by Columbus, he thought at first it was three islands as all he could see was three hills silhouetted against the sky. However, when he got closer, he found that what he had seen was not three islands at all but just one island. From a distance it looked like three, but close up it was only one. Hence he named the island "Trinidad," Spanish for "Trinity."

That is the kind of experience you get when reading the Word of God. At first it seems as if the Bible is talking about three Gods, but as you go deeper into the Scriptures you discover there are not three Gods but one – one God in three Persons.

It must be noted though that it is not only in isolated texts that one encounters the doctrine of the Trinity. The very concept of God's love presupposes plurality in the Godhead. Love, to be love, must have an object. Self-love is love's opposite. Since God (as we shall see more closely in a few days' time) is *eternal* love, He must have had objects of eternal affection. The objects of His affection were the Son and the Spirit. The doctrine of the Trinity, therefore, is not only theologically but logically necessary to an understanding of the nature of the Deity.

FURTHER STUDY

Eph. 4:1–6;
Deut. 4:35
Psa. 83:18
1 Cor. 8:4

1. What did Paul confirm to the Ephesians and the Corinthians?

2. What was the psalmist's conviction?

⊹→ *Prayer* ⊹→

Father, help me understand that a being fully comprehended could not be God. In Your unfathomable depths all my thoughts are drowned. Symbolically I remove my shoes, for I sense I stand on holy ground. Amen.

The great triune God

"Thomas said to him, 'My Lord and my God!' " (v.28)

For reading & meditation – John 20:19–30

*D*r. W. E. Sangster tells the story of following three children out of church. One remarked to the others: "I can't understand all this 'Three in One and One in Three' business." "I can't either," said another child, "but I think of it like this: my mother is Mummy to me, she is Mabel to Daddy, and Mrs. Douglas to lots of other people." Is that the answer? Is it just a question of names? Are we right in finding the doctrine of the Trinity in the text we looked at three days ago (Matt. 28:19), where the word "name" is singular but three names are given – Father, Son and Holy Spirit?

No, that is just part of it; there is much more to it than that. God, we know, is one God. But there stepped into the world one day someone who claimed also to be God. His name was Jesus. He forgave sins, claimed to have existence before Abraham, and accepted worship as His right. Worship, remember, is for God alone. After Jesus was resurrected and returned to heaven He sent back the Holy Spirit, who was also seen as God (2 Cor. 13:14). He – the Holy Spirit – came *into* the disciples and brought with him the resources of the Godhead, breaking the sin in their nature, pleading in prayer, and exalting the Savior.

Thus we see God is One but also Three in One: God above us, God among us, God within us. The Father in majesty, the Son in suffering, the Spirit in striving. This is the central mystery of our most holy faith. Together, and with all our hearts, let us adore the great triune God.

FURTHER STUDY

John 1:1–14; 8:58; 10:30; 17:5

1. How did John describe Jesus?

2. What did Jesus declare of Himself?

⇢ *Prayer* ⇠

Father, Son, and Holy Spirit, though I cannot comprehend Your essential oneness and unity, I can worship You nevertheless. This I do now, in humble adoration. Glory, honor, and power be unto Your Name forever and ever. Amen.

A watershed truth

"... the grace of the Lord Jesus Christ ... the love of God ...
the fellowship of the Holy Spirit ..." (v.14)

For reading & meditation – 2 Corinthians 13:1-14

That great Christian, Francis Schaeffer, said that he would have remained an agnostic if it weren't for the doctrine of the Trinity. It was this, he claimed, that gave him the answer – the only answer – to the theme of unity and diversity.

The question I have been asked most often about the Trinity is this: Why did not God make clear the truth of the Trinity in the Old Testament and not leave it as something to be deduced in the New Testament? I usually answer like this: Before God could entrust His people with the knowledge of His essential Threeness, He had to lay deep in their minds a piercing conviction of His Oneness. The Bible begins in monotheism (belief in one God), but soon after the Fall comes polytheism (belief in many gods) – which god is the real God. Not until belief in one God was laid deep in the consciousness of the Jewish nation was God ready to reveal more clearly to mankind the sublime truth of the Trinity.

Dr. George Smeaton says: "The biblical idea of the Trinity is the heart of the unique message of Christianity. To explain this mystery is not our province ... ours is simply to conserve the mystery." In my experience, those who call themselves Christians but yet reject the doctrine of the Trinity will soon latch onto some other error. It is a strange thing but I have observed it as a fact of the Christian life that when this truth is modified or pushed aside, it is as if the door is opened to the inrush of all kinds of absurd ideas, bizarre theories, and half-truths.

FURTHER STUDY

John 14:8–21; 17:22

1. How did Jesus depict the Trinity?

2. What did Jesus confirm?

↞⊷ *Prayer* ⊶↠

Father, help me hold fast to this sublime truth, and enable me to see that though something is above reason, it is not necessarily against reason. Blessed Trinity, Father, Son, and Holy Spirit, I worship You. Amen.

The high-water mark

"God is love." (v.16)

For reading & meditation – 1 John 4:7-16

*W*e turn now to consider another aspect of God's nature and character – *love*. There are three things told us in Scripture concerning the nature of God. First, "God is *spirit*" (John 4:24), which means He has no visible substance. Second, "God is *light*" (1 John 1:5), which means no darkness can dwell in Him. In Scripture darkness stands for sin, death, and so on. Third, "God is *love*," which means that the energy that flows out from His Being is that of infinite, eternal beneficence.

When John wrote the words "God is love" it was no slick statement, as it was the first time in history that the phrase had been used in that way. People had believed that God was love, and had speculated about His benevolence, but now the categorical statement is laid down for all to behold. These words, in my judgment, are the high-water mark of divine revelation; nothing more needs to be said for nothing greater can be said.

I often create a mental picture for myself of the angels peering over the battlements of heaven as John wrote those words and then, when they had been written down, I imagine them breaking into rapturous applause and saying to each other: "They've got it. They've got it! At last they see that God is love." And a sigh of deep satisfaction and great joy would have filled the portals of heaven in the knowledge that the greatest truth about God was now made crystal clear. The implied was now inscribed.

FURTHER STUDY

Jer. 31:1-4;
John 3:16;
Rom. 5:8

1. What did the Lord appear and say?

2. How did He demonstrate this?

❧ *Prayer* ❧

O Father, I am so thankful that You have demonstrated categorically that the greatest thing about You is love. My heart gladly rests upon that glorious fact. I look forward to exploring it forever. Amen.

Amazing love!

*"The Lord did not ... choose you because you were ... numerous
... But the Lord loved you ..." (vv.7–8)*

For reading & meditation – Deuteronomy 7:1–10

When the Bible says God *is* love, it is saying more than that God loves, or that God is loving, or even that God is lovely; it is saying that love is the power behind everything He does – love is not merely one of His attributes but His whole nature. God is not only the Author of loving acts; He is love in the very core of His Being. Our thoughts of God's love must be built on God's revelation about Himself in the Scriptures, not by projecting our own ideas about love on to Him. Let's focus, therefore, on what the Bible has to say about the God who is love.

First, God's love is *uninfluenced*. By that I mean nothing in us can give rise to it and nothing in us can extinguish it. It is "love for nothing," as someone once put it. The love which we humans have for one another is drawn out of us by something in the object of our love. But God's love is not like that; His love is free, spontaneous, and uncaused. The passage before us today makes clear that there is no reason behind the love of God for His people. If you look for a reason you just won't find one. He loves because ... He loves.

No man or woman can ever explain *why* God loves us. To "explain" it would require that He loves us for something outside of Himself, and, as we have seen, He loves us for ourselves alone. And that love has its beginning not in us but in Himself. He is love's source as well as its river.

FURTHER STUDY

Eph. 2:1–10;
1 John 3:1

1. How does Paul describe God's reason for saving us?

2. How does John put it?

⊷ *Prayer* ⊷

O God, what security this gives me to know that Your love for me will never be diminished and never be taken away. Help me reflect on this and draw from it the inspiration I need to walk tall and strong through every day. In Jesus' Name. Amen.

What a tranquilizer!

"I have loved you with an everlasting love ..." (v.3)

For reading & meditation – Jeremiah 31:1–12

"How little real love there is for God," says theologian Arthur W. Pink. He suggests that this and the resulting low level of spirituality in today's Church are caused by our hearts being so little occupied with thoughts of the divine love. "The better we are acquainted with His love," he says, "– its character, its fullness, its blessedness – the more will our hearts be drawn out in love to Him." We focus now on the fact that God's love is *eternal*.

God being eternal, it follows that His love also is eternal. This means that God loved us before earth and heaven were called into existence, that He has set His heart upon us from all eternity. This is the truth set forth in Ephesians 1:4–5 where we are told that we were chosen in Christ before the foundation of the world. What a tranquilizer this is for our hearts! If God's love for you had no beginning then it has no ending either. It is from "everlasting to everlasting."

Another thing we need to know about the love of God is that it is a *holy* love. This means that His love is not regulated by whim, or caprice, or sentiment, but by principle. Just as His grace reigns not at the expense of righteousness but "through" it (Rom. 5:21), so His love never conflicts with His holiness. This is why John says that God is *light* before he says God is *love*. And this is why, too, the Almighty never lets us get away with anything. He loves us too much for that. His love is pure, holy and unmixed with maudlin sentimentality. God will not wink at sin, not even in His own people.

FURTHER STUDY

Rom. 8:18–39;
1 Pet. 1:17–21

1. What was Paul convinced of?

2. How does Peter portray the eternal perspective?

⊷ *Prayer* ⊷

O Father, the more I learn about Your love the more my heart is set on fire. Increase my understanding, for I see that the more I comprehend how much I am loved the more secure I am in that love. Amen.

Love creating love

"We love because he first loved us." (v.19)
For reading & meditation – 1 John 4:17–21; 5:1–12

Although the love of God is clearly laid out in the Old Testament, why did humankind have to wait so long to have the message spelled out in such clear terms as John uses: *God is love?* People could not see this sufficiently clearly until they had looked into the face of Jesus. In the life of Jesus is the clearest revelation that God is love.

So few of us open ourselves to the love of God. We have more fear of Him than we have love for Him. There is, of course, a godly fear (or reverence), but that is not what I mean. If we fail to comprehend how much we are loved by God, then there will be no energy to turn the machinery of our lives in the way they were meant to turn.

When I was a young Christian, whenever I doubted the love of God I was told I should go to Calvary. I never quite understood what that meant until one day I complained to God that He couldn't really love me; if He did, He wouldn't let such things happen as were befalling me. He gave me no answer but showed me the Cross. And as I saw His Son dying there for me, the scales fell from my eyes and I found love for Him flowing out of His love for me. I discovered what the verse at the top of this page meant: "We love *because* he first loved us."

Love for God is not the fruit of labor but the response of our hearts to being loved. It is not something we manufacture; it is something we receive.

FURTHER STUDY

John 19:16–30;
Eph. 2:15–16;
Col. 1:19–22

1. What is the result of the Cross?

2. Spend some moments in prayer contemplating the Cross.

⋙ *Prayer* ⋘

O God my Father, save me from believing that my problem is I don't love You enough, when the real problem is I don't know how much I am loved by You. Let the scales fall from my eyes right now and let me see – really see. In Jesus' Name. Amen.

The Cross's magnetism

*"But I, when I am lifted up from the earth, will draw
all men to myself." (v.32)*

For reading & meditation – John 12:20–33

he love for God that burns in our hearts must never be
seen as the fruit of our labor, as if it is something we
manufacture. Seeing the love of God for us, our own heart
responds with love. We give love for love. We cannot help it. Let's
be done with the idea that love for God is something we work at.
It issues forth in good works, of course, but it *begins* in
contemplation of how much we are loved.

I often tell my students that they cannot love until they have
been loved. By this I mean that love is a response. Our souls must
receive love before they can give out love. Those who did not
receive much love from their parents complain at this stage: "I
can't love God because my soul was never properly prepared to
love; my parents didn't love me." That is a problem I agree, but it
must never be seen as an insoluble problem. No one who stands
at Calvary and sees God dying for them on that tree can ever argue
that because they were not loved by their parents they cannot now
receive God's love. If they really believe that, then they are saying
that God's love is balked by the adverse influence of human
conditioning.

God's love will only flow into us if we let it, and if we really want
it. To desire it is like the touch of the hand on a spring blind; the
blind is released and the sunlight flows in. Just to *want* His love is
enough; He will do the rest.

FURTHER STUDY

2 Thess. 3:1–5;
Jude v.21;
Eph. 3:17–19

1. What was Paul's
desire for the
Thessalonians?

2. What was Paul's
prayer for the
Ephesians?

⟶ *Prayer* ⟵

*O God, forgive me if I have used excuses to barricade my heart against Your love.
I gaze once more on Calvary and open my heart to allow its mighty magnetism
to draw my soul toward You in a way it has never been drawn before. In Jesus'
Name. Amen.*

The quality par excellence

"Holy, holy, holy is the Lord Almighty ..." (v.3)

For reading & meditation – Isaiah 6:1–13

The next aspect of God's nature and character we examine is that of His *holiness*. Even the most casual reader of the Scriptures cannot help but notice that God is portrayed in the Bible as uniquely and awesomely holy. In fact, there are more references to the holiness of God in Scripture than to any other aspect of His character. This ought to give us some indication of how important it is.

But what do we mean when we say God is "holy"? There are three thoughts underlying the word "holy." First, the idea of separation, being withdrawn or apart. Second, brightness or brilliance. Third, moral majesty, purity, or cleanliness. It is interesting that those who came into direct contact with the Almighty in the Old Testament were inevitably overwhelmed by His moral majesty.

Isaiah went into the Temple to pray at a time when his people were in grave difficulties. Uzziah, the king who had ruled for half a century, was dying and Assyria, a terrible and evil force, stood threateningly to the north. I feel sure that whatever answer Isaiah thought he would get as he opened up his heart to God, it was not the one he received. He was given a vision of a holy God that shook him to the core of his being. Why should this be? I think it was because the concept of God's holiness is the *main* lesson in His school, the divine prerequisite for admission to the inner heart of God, the most important qualification for learning from the Lord.

FURTHER STUDY

Ex. 15:1–11;
Psa. 99:9

1. What question did Moses pose?

2. What did the psalmist affirm?

→ *Prayer* ←

Father, I must search my heart this day and ask myself: Do I know what it is to serve a holy God? Have I ever received a vision of the moral majesty and purity of the Divine? Deepen my understanding of all this I pray. In Jesus' Name. Amen.

A prod toward perfection

*"... what does the Lord your God ask of you but to fear
the Lord your God ...?" (v.12)*

For reading & meditation – Deuteronomy 10:12–22

The *first* thing God called Israel to do when He announced that they were to be His special people and live the way He wanted them to live, was to *fear* Him. Loving Him, serving Him and keeping His laws were of great importance, of course, but the very first things God asks of them are reverence and fear.

How does all this relate to the love of God? When thinking about God, it is wise to see love and holiness as intertwined; not to do so can lead sometimes to serious error. Many in today's Church present the love of God in such a way that it has given rise to the saying "God loves me as I am." The idea in many minds is: "God loves me as I am, and whether I go on from here or whether I stay the same, it makes no difference to His love for me." This is entirely true, but it is not the entire truth. Because God is love, He loves us as we are, but because He is *holy* love, He loves us too much to let us stay as we are. We can be secure in the fact that God loves us just the way we are, but the holy love of God calls us to move ever closer to Him and cries out: "Be holy as I am holy."

Error is truth out of balance. We need to rejoice in the fact that we are loved because of who we are and not for what we do, but we must see also that God's love is a holy love and thus will *inevitably* prod us toward perfection.

FURTHER STUDY
1 Sam. 6:1–21;
Rev. 15:4
1. What question did the men of Beth Shemesh ask?
2. What truth had been revealed to John in the song of the Lamb?

⊷ *Prayer* ⊷

O Father, help me keep these two things in balance. Don't let the security I feel as I rest in Your love turn to smugness and complacency. Show me that though I am "accepted in the Beloved," that does not mean You don't want me to come closer. Amen.

The consuming fire

"... our 'God is a consuming fire.' " (v.29)
For reading & meditation – Hebrews 12:14–29

George MacDonald writes: "Nothing is inexorable but love ... For love loves unto purity. Love has ever in view the absolute loveliness of that which it beholds. Where loveliness is incomplete, and love cannot love its fill of loving, it spends itself to make more lovely, that it may love more; it strives for perfection even that itself may be perfected – not in itself but in the object. Therefore all that is not beautiful in the beloved, all that comes between and is not of love's kind, must be destroyed. *Our God is a consuming fire.*" Powerful words.

The nature of God is so terribly pure that it destroys everything that is not as pure as fire. God desires us to worship Him in "the beauty of holiness." This means that He wants the purity in us to match the purity in Him. We cannot arrive at this purity by self-effort, of course, but the more we draw nigh to Him the more the fire of His purity will burn out the dross within us.

"It is not the fire will burn us up if we do not worship," said George MacDonald, "but the fire will burn us up *until* we worship." And the fire will go on burning within us after everything that is foreign to it has been consumed, no longer with pain and a sense of something unwanted being consumed, but as the highest consciousness of life. God is a *consuming* fire. He always was, and always will be – world without end.

FURTHER STUDY

Psa. 97:1–5;
Isa. 66:15;
1 Cor. 3:12–14

1. What does the psalmist say about fire?

2. What will the fire do?

→ *Prayer* ←

O God, I long with all my heart that my worship might be all You want it to be. May Your consuming fire burn out all the dross within me until everything that is foreign to Your nature is part of me no more. In Jesus' Name I ask it. Amen.

The fear of God

"To fear the Lord is to hate evil ..." (v.13)
For reading & meditation – Proverbs 8:1–21

e are taught over and over again in Scripture that because God is uniquely and awesomely holy – pure, separated, and shining in His moral majesty – we are to draw near to Him with godly reverence and fear.

The fear of the Lord (we said the other day) is the beginning of wisdom. Contemplation of His character, particularly His holiness, will lead to a reverential fear that prepares the soul (as it did for Isaiah) for more profitable service and activity. But what does it mean to "fear" God? There are times in the Bible when we are told to fear, and times when we are told *not* to fear. There is a fear that helps and a fear that hinders. How do we know the difference?

The fear that helps is the fear that expresses itself in reverence, veneration, awe, a sense of grandeur and majesty of God. The fear that hinders is described for us in 2 Timothy 1:7: "For God did not give us a spirit of timidity, but a spirit of power, of love and of self-discipline." The Greek word *deilia*, which is translated "timidity" in this verse, comes from a root that means "wretched, sorry, miserable" and implies someone lacking in courage. God is not to blame for attitudes of cowardice or timidity; they come from within our own hearts. Timid people are frightened people, and if you want to explore this thought still further ask yourself: What kinds of things frighten me that are not related to the fear of God? If we fear them more than we fear God then we are being ruled by the wrong kind of fear.

FURTHER STUDY

Deut. 10:1–12;
Josh. 24:14;
Eccl. 12:13

1. What did the Lord require of Israel?

2. What did Joshua admonish Israel to do?

✦ *Prayer* ✦

O God, I bring all those fears within me that hinder to You right now and lay them at Your feet. Help me develop such a reverential fear for You that all other fears are quickly swallowed up. In Jesus' Name. Amen.

The power of holiness

*"Exalt the Lord our God and worship at his footstool;
he is holy." (v.5)*

For reading & meditation – Psalm 99:1–9

N o one can know the true grace of God," said the great Bible teacher A. W. Tozer, "who has not first known the fear of God." He continued: "Always there was about any manifestation of God something that dismayed the onlookers, that daunted and overawed them ... I do not believe any lasting good can come from religious activities that are not rooted in this fear. Until we have been gripped by that nameless terror which results when an unholy creature is suddenly confronted by the One who is holiest of all, we are not likely to be affected by the doctrine of love and grace."

There was a time when the nature and character of God was a constant theme in Christian pulpits, but not any more. Generally speaking, today's preachers (and writers) tend to give people what they want rather than what they need. This is why we must stop every time we come across a reference to God's character in our Bibles and pause to consider it. No one has done anything mighty for God without a new vision of God's holiness. Ezekiel tells us of the "rims" in his vision that were so high (Ezek. 1:18) they were "awesome," and Jacob, rising from his sleep, said: "How awesome is this place!" (Gen. 28:17).

We will be of little use to God unless we know how to tremble before Him, for otherwise our own ideas and feelings of self-sufficiency will soon take over. Have we lost the sense of awe when we come into God's presence which seemed to characterise the saints of the past? I am afraid we have.

FURTHER STUDY

Ex. 3:1–5;
Josh. 5:15;
Psa. 33:8; 89:7

1. What was Moses' and Joshua's experience?

2. What did the psalmist admonish?

⊷ *Prayer* ⊷

---

*O God, I am afraid as I draw near to You, but I draw near because I am afraid.
Nothing or no one can dissolve the fears that hinder me but You. Draw me closer,
for in You and You alone lies both my salvation and sanctification. Amen.*

Our trustworthy God

*"... he is the faithful God, keeping his covenant of love
to a thousand generations ..." (v.9)*

For reading & meditation – Deuteronomy 7:7–20

e move on now to consider another aspect of God's character – His abiding faithfulness. God is utterly trustworthy in all He says and does, and this is the rock-bottom reality on which everything in the universe depends. In an age when so much unfaithfulness abounds, how good it is to realize that we have One who will never let us down, never have to apologise for failing us, and never go back on His Word.

Am I speaking to someone who has just discovered unfaithfulness in a marriage partner, or experienced the break-up of a relationship because a person you trusted did not keep their word? It's a sad moment when we get a revelation of the inconsistency of the human heart. But we need to look into our own hearts also, for none of us can claim complete immunity to the sin of unfaithfulness. We may not have broken a contract or violated the marriage covenant but we have been unfaithful to Christ in other ways – to the light and privileges which God has entrusted to us, perhaps.

How refreshing it is, then, to read today's text and focus our gaze on the One who is faithful at all times and in all things. We may let Him down but He will never let us down. A chorus I learned as a young Christian comes back to me time and time again when I am tempted to doubt the faithfulness of God:

FURTHER STUDY
1 Kings 8:54–61;
Psa. 89:1–8
1. What did Solomon testify?
2. What did the psalmist promise to do?

> *He cannot fail for He is God,*
> *He cannot fail, He pledged His Word,*
> *He cannot fail, He'll see you through,*
> *He cannot fail, He'll answer you.*

⊷ *Prayer* ⊶

Gracious and loving God, what inspiration it brings to my soul to realize that of all the things You can do, the one thing You can't do is fail. May the reality of this be the pavement on which I tread this day and every day. In Jesus' Name. Amen.

Great is Thy faithfulness

*"Your love, O Lord, reaches to the heavens, your
faithfulness to the skies." (v.5)*

For reading & meditation – Psalm 36:1–12

ow wonderful it is, in an age where unfaithfulness abounds, to focus our gaze on those Scriptures that point to the trustworthiness of our God. The one before us today is quite wonderful, but consider also these: "O Lord God Almighty, who is like you? You are mighty, O Lord, and your faithfulness surrounds you" (Psa. 89:8); "Righteousness will be his belt and faithfulness the sash round his waist" (Isa. 11:5); "If we are faithless, he will remain faithful, for he cannot disown himself" (2 Tim. 2:13). Can't you just feel the energy that flows from these Scriptures buttressing your confidence in God? For God to be unfaithful would be to act contrary to His nature, and if He ever was (we are only speculating because He could never do so) then He would cease to be God.

Focus again with me on the text at the top of the page. We are told God's faithfulness extends to the skies. This is the psalmist's picturesque way of expressing the fact that far above all finite comprehension is the unchanging faithfulness of God. Everything about God is vast and incomparable, including His faithfulness. He never forgets a thing, never makes a mistake, never fails to keep a promise, never falters over a decision, never retracts a statement He has made, and has never breached a contract. Every declaration He has made, every promise He has given, every covenant He has struck is vouchsafed by His faithful character. This is why Christians all around the world can say with confidence: "... his compassions never fail. They are new every morning; *great* is your faithfulness" (Lam. 3:22–23).

FURTHER STUDY

1 Cor. 1:1–9;
Heb. 6:18;
1 Pet. 4:19

1. What did Paul assure the Corinthians?

2. What is it impossible for God to do?

✦✦ *Prayer* ✦✦

O God, how great Thou art. Great in power, great in majesty, great in love, great in mercy – great in so many things. But above all you are great in faithfulness. How I rejoice in that. Amen.

The need to know

"Let us hold unswervingly to the hope we profess, for he who promised is faithful." (v.23)

For reading & meditation – Hebrews 10:19–31

The Bible is a veritable mine of information on the fact of God's faithfulness. More than 4,000 years ago He said: "As long as the earth endures, seedtime and harvest, cold and heat, summer and winter, day and night will never cease" (Gen. 8:22). Every year furnishes us with fresh evidence that He has not gone back on His Word.

In Genesis 15:13–14 God declared to Abraham: "Know for certain that your descendants will be strangers in a country not their own, and they will be enslaved and ill-treated four hundred years. But ... afterwards they will come out with great possessions." Did that happen? Exodus 12:41 says: "At the end of the 430 years, to the very day, all the Lord's divisions left Egypt." The prophet Isaiah predicted that a virgin should conceive and bear a son whose name would be Immanuel (Isa. 7:14). Centuries later the prediction came to pass. In Galatians 4:4 we read: "But when the time had fully come, God sent his Son, born of a woman ...."

I wish I had the space to take you through the pages of Scripture and show you how faithful God has been to His Word. But you have a Bible for yourself; study it. Read it to know God. It is absolutely imperative that we who live in an age when unfaithfulness abounds, should acquaint ourselves with the fact of God's faithfulness. This is the basis of our confidence in Him. And this is why the Bible fairly bulges with this great and gripping truth. The more of God's truth we pack into our souls, the better equipped we are for the road that lies ahead.

FURTHER STUDY

Mal.3:7;
Psa. 103:17; 102:27;
James 1:1–17

1. What did the Lord declare to Israel?

2. How did James put it?

✦ *Prayer* ✦

Gracious and loving Father, the more I learn about Your nature and character the more I want to know. Just these glimpses I am getting set my soul on fire to know You more intimately. Take me deeper, dear Lord. In Jesus' Name. Amen.

"Standing on the promises"

"... he has given us his very great and precious promises ..." (v.4)

For reading & meditation – 2 Peter 1:1–11

*I*t is one thing to accept the faithfulness of God as a clear biblical truth; it is quite another to act upon it. God has given us many great and precious promises, as our text for today puts it, but do we actually count on them being fulfilled?

We have to be careful that we do not hold God to promises He has not given. I have seen a good deal of heartache suffered by Christians because someone encouraged them to take a statement from the Word of God, turn it into a "promise," and urged them to believe for it to come to pass. Then, when nothing happened, they became deeply discouraged. One woman told me that many years ago she had taken the words found in Acts 16:31 – "Believe in the Lord Jesus, and you will be saved – you and your household" – and claimed them as a promise. When her husband and son died unrepentant she was devastated. I pointed out to her that even God cannot save those who don't want to be saved, and that the promise given by Paul and Silas was for the Philippian jailer, not anyone else.

FURTHER STUDY

Heb. 1:1–12; 13:8;
2 Cor. 4:18

1. Why is Jesus so dependable?

2. Where do we fix our eyes?

There are hundreds of promises that God has given in His Word that we can claim without equivocation. "I will never leave thee, nor forsake thee" (Heb. 13:5, KJV) is just one among many. Someone who has counted all God's promises in the Bible numbers them as being over 3,000. That ought to be enough to keep you going if you lived to be a hundred. Be careful, however, that it is a *general* promise you are banking on, not a *specific* one.

✦⊰ *Prayer* ⊱✦

Father, I have Your promise that You will guide me into all truth, so my trust is in You that You will give me the wisdom to discern between a promise which is general and one that is specific. In Jesus' Name. Amen.

He can't forget!

Jesus answered, 'The work of God is this: to believe in the one he has sent.'" (v.29)

For reading & meditation – John 6:25–33

*I*t is because God is so utterly trustworthy and reliable that the Christian life at heart is a life of trust. In the passage before us today our Lord is asked: "What must we do to do the works God requires?" (v.28). His answer was entirely different from that which you would receive if you posed the question to adherents of different religious systems today. A Buddhist would answer: "We must follow the eightfold path of Buddhism." A Muslim would answer: "We must fast and pray and make a trip to Mecca." Some followers of the Christian way might answer "We must engage in regular Bible study, prayer, tithing and Christian fellowship." But the answer Jesus gave was this: "The work of God is this: *to believe ...*"

George Watson, a devotional writer, said: "To trust the Origin of our existence is the fundamental grace of life. There is one virtue [in God] that stands out forever more conspicuously than friendship, or love, or knowledge, or wisdom ... it is fidelity. *God's fidelity is in Him what trust is in us*" (emphasis mine). Understanding that God is utterly trustworthy will deliver us from such incapacitating emotions as worry, anxiety and fear. To be overwhelmed by the concerns of this life reflects poorly upon the faithfulness of God.

An old saint who was dying became concerned that he couldn't remember any of God's promises. His pastor said: "Do you think that God will forget any of them?" A smile came over the face of the dying Christian as he exclaimed joyfully: "No, no, He won't." That too is our confidence. He *won't* forget, because being God, He *can't* forget.

FURTHER STUDY

2 Tim. 2:1–13;
Heb. 2:17, 10:23

1. What did Paul assure Timothy?

2. Why was Jesus made like His brothers?

 Prayer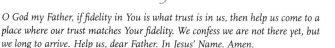

O God my Father, if fidelity in You is what trust is in us, then help us come to a place where our trust matches Your fidelity. We confess we are not there yet, but we long to arrive. Help us, dear Father. In Jesus' Name. Amen.

No blemish in God

"... I will take vengeance on my adversaries and repay those who hate me." (v.41)

For reading & meditation – Deuteronomy 32:36–47

We turn now to focus on an aspect of God's character which for some reason many see as a blotch or blemish in the divine nature. I refer to the matter of God's *wrath*. Though the subject may be missing from many modern-day pulpits, it is not missing from the Bible. If you look up in a Bible concordance all the texts that refer to the wrath, anger or the severity of God, you will find that there are more references to these than there are to His love, graciousness or tenderness. A proper study of God can never be complete unless consideration is given to the fact that God is not only a God of love but a God of wrath and anger also.

I remember in the early days of my Christian experience that whenever I heard any reference to the wrath of God I would feel a deep resentment arise within me, and instead of regarding this aspect of God's nature with delight, I looked upon it with disdain. Later, however, when I came to understand it and saw it in its proper light – as something to rejoice in rather than to be resented – I found my love for God and my awe of God swell to new proportions.

Arthur W. Pink describes the wrath of God as the "eternal detestation of all unrighteousness ... the displeasure and indignation of divine equity against evil ... the holiness of God stirred into activity against sin." *Never* view the wrath of God as a moral blemish or a blotch on His character. It would be a blemish if wrath were absent from Him.

FURTHER STUDY

2 Kings 22:1–13;
Psa. 90:11

1. Why did God's anger burn?
2. What did the psalmist say about God's wrath?

⊷⊶ *Prayer* ⊷⊶

Father, I would face all reality – even those aspects that do not fit into my preconceived ideas. Help me not to balk at the idea that You are a God of wrath as well as a God of wonder. In Jesus' Name I pray. Amen.

"God's great intolerance"

*"... they have rejected the law of the Lord Almighty ...
Therefore the Lord's anger burns ..." (vv.24–25)*

For reading & meditation – Isaiah 5:18–25

e pick up from where we left off yesterday with the thought that "wrath" is not a defect in the divine character; rather, it would be a defect if wrath were absent from Him. Those who see God's wrath as petulance or retaliation, inflicting punishment for the sake of it, or in return for some injury received, do not really understand it. Divine wrath is not vindictiveness; it is divine perfection and issues forth from God because it is right.

Human beings tend to make God in our own image. He made us in His image but we want to return the compliment, and it is there that so often we go wrong. Instead of reasoning from the divine down to the human, and recognizing that sin has marred the divine image within us, we reason from our fallen condition and project our own feelings and ideas onto God. Thus, when thinking of the wrath of God, we tend to look at what happens in our own hearts when we get angry and imagine God to be the same. Divine anger must never be confused with human anger. Most of what goes on in our hearts whenever we are angry is a mixture of unpredictable petulance, retaliation, hostility, and self-concern. God's anger is always predictable, always steadfast, and always set against sin. We must never forget that God's nature is *uncompromisingly* set against sin. We may tolerate it; He never.

Sin has been defined as "God's one great intolerance," and for that we ought to be eternally grateful. As His children we ought to rejoice that He will not tolerate anything harmful to us.

FURTHER STUDY

Psa. 5:1–6; 11:5;
Hab. 1:12–13;
Zech. 8:16–17

1. How did the psalmist express God's great intolerance?

2. What does the Lord hate?

→ *Prayer* ←

O Father, what a change comes over me when I realize Your wrath is not so much directed at persons but at the sin that demeans and destroys them. You are not against me for my sin, but for me against my sin. I am deeply, deeply grateful. Amen.

Righteous indignation

*"The wrath of God is being revealed ... against all the
godlessness and wickedness of men ..." (v.18)*

For reading & meditation – Romans 1:8–25

For many of us "wrath" conjures up the idea of being out of control, an outburst of "seeing red," a sense of wounded pride or just downright petulance. It is quite wrong to take those ideas or feelings and impose them on God. God's wrath is never out of control, never capricious, never self-indulgent, never irritable, and never ignoble. These may be predicated of human anger but never of the divine. God is angry only when anger is called for. Even among men and women there is such a thing as righteous indignation, though (in my opinion) it is more rare than we think. I used to believe the difference between righteous indignation and carnal hostility was this: when someone was angry with me *that* was carnal hostility; when I was angry with someone else *that* was righteous indignation! I have "grown out" of that opinion now, I hasten to add. All God's indignation is righteous. It is grief at what is happening to others, not a grudge because of what is happening to Him.

Would a God who took as much pleasure in evil as He did in good be a God we could love? Would a God who did not react adversely to evil be morally perfect? Of course not. It is precisely this adverse reaction to evil that the Bible has in mind when it talks about God's wrath. God cannot treat good and evil alike. He can look over it – look over it to the Cross where it can be forgiven – but He cannot overlook it.

FURTHER STUDY

Isa. 13:1–22;
Psa. 78:40–55;
Isa. 30:27

1. How does the psalmist describe the outworking of God's wrath?

2. How did Isaiah depict God's anger toward Babylon?

✦ *Prayer* ✦

O God, the more I see the reason behind Your wrath, and the more I consider the purity of its motive, the more praise and adoration I want to give. What a great and wonderful God You are. And how glad I am that You looked over my sin. Amen.

The unyielding Judge

"Settle matters quickly with your adversary who is taking you to court." (v.25)

For reading & meditation – Matthew 5:21–26

"God's wrath," said George MacDonald, "is always *judicial*. It is always the wrath of the Judge administering justice. Cruelty is always immoral but true justice – never." Those who experience the fullness of God's wrath get precisely what they deserve. That may sound hard, but it is true.

There is great wisdom in the words of our Lord in the passage before us today. Settle matters with an adversary, He says, before he drags you to court. Do at once what you must do one day. As there is no escape from payment, escape at least from the prison sentence that will enforce it. The point our Lord is making is that we ought not to drive justice to extremities. God requires righteousness of us. It is utterly useless to think we can escape the eternal law. Yield yourself rather than be compelled.

To those whose hearts are true, the idea of judgment is right; to those whose hearts are untrue, the idea of judgment is wrong. Many people live under the illusion that perhaps it might be possible to find a way of escaping all that is required of us in this world. But there is no escape. A way to avoid the demands of righteousness, apart from the righteousness which God accounts to us at the Cross, would not be moral. When a man or woman accepts the payment God has made for them in Christ, the whole wealth of heaven is theirs; their debt is cleared. Those who deny that debt, or acknowledging it do nothing to avail themselves of the payment made on Calvary, must face at last an unyielding Judge and an everlasting prison.

FURTHER STUDY

Zeph. 3:1–5;
Psa. 103:6;
John 5:30;
Rom. 2:2

1. What does God do morning by morning?

2. What is God's judgment based on?

⊷ *Prayer* ⊷

O Father, how serious and solemn is all this – but yet how true. Sin must ultimately be punished. I am so grateful that You have shown me that in Christ my debt has been paid, and availing myself of Your offer I am eternally free. Blessed be Your Name forever. Amen.

Heaven or hell

*"In hell, where he was in torment, he looked up
and saw Abraham far away ..." (v.23)*

For reading & meditation – Luke 16:19–31

The final state of those who die without availing themselves of the forgiveness God offers them at the Cross is eternal banishment from God's presence. The Bible calls this "hell." "There is no heaven with a little hell in it," said George MacDonald, meaning that the God who is passionately for righteousness and implacably against sin must ensure that the two are finally separated.

However, hell is always something that people choose for themselves. It is a state for which men and women opt. Before hell is experienced as eternal, it is always experienced as something temporary in the sense that as men and women retreat from the light God shines into their hearts to lead them to Himself, they experience in a small way what they will experience in full when they are banished into "outer darkness" (Matt. 25:30, KJV). Dorothy Sayers described hell as "the enjoyment of one's own way forever." God says to those who die impenitent: "You preferred your own way to mine; you shall have it – forever." In the last analysis, all that God does in consigning people to hell is to allow them to face the full consequences of the choice they have made. God is resolute in punishing sin, and hell is the final consequence of this.

I know most of my readers are Christians, but I know also some are not. Those of you reading these lines who have never surrendered your lives to Christ, I urge you to surrender your hearts to Him today. Christ has died to save you from hell. Pray this prayer with me now.

FURTHER STUDY

Matt. 5:27–30; 18:7–9;
25:34–43

1. How did Jesus illustrate the importance of avoiding hell?

2. How can we be sure of avoiding hell?

✦ Prayer ✦

Father God, I come to You now through Your Son, the Lord Jesus Christ. I repent of my sin, ask Your forgiveness, and receive You into my life as Savior and Lord. Thank You, dear Lord. Amen.

"Love with a 'stoop'"

*"Let us then approach the throne of grace
with confidence ..." (v.16)*

For reading & meditation – Hebrews 4:1–16

We turn now to consider that facet of God's character which we describe as "grace." Grace is more than a synonym for love; it is a characteristic of the Deity which is quite close to love (and mercy) but yet deserves to be seen as different and distinctive.

I heard an old Welsh preacher say: "Grace is a word with a 'stoop' in it; love reaches out on the same level, but grace always has to stoop to pick one up." It was probably this same thought that an anonymous writer had in mind when he said: "Grace is love at its loveliest, falling on the unlovable and making it lovely." But it is to the great Puritan preacher Thomas Goodwin we must turn for the best clarification of the difference between love and grace: "Grace is more than mercy and love. It superadds to them. It denotes not simply love but love of a *sovereign*, transcendently superior One that may do what He will, that may freely choose whether He will love or no. There may be love between equals, and an inferior may love a superior, but love in a Superior, and so superior that He may do what He will, in such a One love is called grace. Grace is attributed to princes; they are said to be 'gracious' to their subjects whereas subjects cannot be gracious to princes."

Grace then is God's kindness bestowed upon the undeserving; benevolence handed down to those who have no merit; a hand reaching down to those who have fallen into a pit. The Bible bids us believe that on the throne of the universe there is a God like that.

FURTHER STUDY

Dan. 9:1–18;
Deut. 9:5;
1 Pet. 5:5

1. Is grace the result of righteousness?

2. Who does God give grace to?

⊹⟶ *Prayer* ⟵⊹

Loving and gracious God, help me understand more deeply than ever what it means to be a recipient of Your grace. I have some idea but I long to realize it even more. Help me, my Father. In Jesus' Name. Amen.

Amazing!

*"So too, at the present time there is a remnant
chosen by grace." (v.5)*

For reading & meditation – Romans 11:1–24

We continue reflecting on the meaning of grace. Illion T. Jones, a famous Welsh preacher, said that "The word 'grace' is unquestionably the most significant single word in the Bible."

I agree. But it must be understood right away that grace is a characteristic of God which is exercized only toward those who are seen as having a special relationship with Him. Nowhere in the Bible is the grace of God ever mentioned in connection with humankind generally, though some theologians frequently use the term "common grace" (a term not mentioned in the Bible) – the idea that God gives a special form of grace to the whole of humankind which restrains them from being as bad as they could be. The other day I came across a writer who said: "The creation of the universe was an exercise of grace." I understand that he might have been using the word "grace" as a synonym for love (a mistake often made by Christian writers), but strictly speaking the exhibition of grace is reserved for the elect – those God foreknew would be brought into a special relationship with Himself through His Son, Jesus Christ. This is why we must distinguish "grace" from "mercy" or "goodness," for Scripture says: "The Lord is good to *all*, And His tender mercies are over *all* his works" (Psa. 145:9, NKJV).

Arthur W. Pink says: "Grace is the sole source from which flows the goodwill, love and salvation of God into His *chosen* people." Grace cannot be bought, earned, deserved, or merited. If it could, it would cease to be grace. Grace flows down as pure charity, "falling on the unlovable and making it lovely." Amazing!

FURTHER STUDY

Rom. 3:1–24;
Acts 15:11;
2 Tim. 2:1

1. What is the result of responding to God's grace?

2. What was Paul's exhortation to Timothy?

⊷ *Prayer* ⊷

Yes Father, it's truly amazing! That love should stoop down to me – an undeserving, even hell-deserving sinner – such an exhibition of grace is more than I can comprehend. But I receive it nevertheless. And because of it I am saved. Hallelujah!

Sovereign grace

"For it is by grace you have been saved, through faith ...
it is the gift of God ..." (v.8)

For reading & meditation – Ephesians 2:1–10

We are acknowledging that in order to understand "grace" we must see it in relation to a Sovereign. As one writer puts it: "Grace is bound to be sovereign since it cannot by its very nature be subject to compulsion." That is why we often refer to it as *free* grace. There is no reason for grace but grace.

I believe the old definition of grace cannot be improved: "Grace is the free unmerited favor of God." At the heart of all true communion with God there lies this gripping truth – God took the initiative. He is more inclined toward us than we are toward Him. We cannot earn His affection. We have simply to receive it. Always the initiative is from God. When you originally came to Him you came because He first drew you. The very faith by which you lay hold of Him is not of yourself; it is, as our text says, "the *gift* of God." Every step you make on your spiritual pilgrimage is possible because of His grace.

I know this teaching affronts modern-day men and women because they like to feel that they can "work their passage to heaven," as one preacher puts it. That is like someone in debt for a million pounds trying to get the one to whom he is indebted to accept his resources of a few pence as being sufficient to clear the debt. Listen to the Word of God again and let it sink deep into your soul: "For it is by *grace* you have been saved ... it is the *gift* of God." Grace is a gift. You have not to achieve but simply receive.

FURTHER STUDY

**Rom. 5:1–21;
Titus 3:7**

1. How does Paul define grace?

2. Write out your own definition of grace.

✦ *Prayer* ✦

O Father, once again my heart is moved as I realize it was not my merit but Your mercy, acting in grace, that drew You to me, and me to you. All honor and glory be to Your mighty and everlasting Name. Amen.

"We've won a holiday"

*"In him we have ... the forgiveness of sins, in accordance
with the riches of God's grace ..." (v.7)*

For reading & meditation – Ephesians 1:1–14

What is it in the heart of most men and women that rejects the idea of God's free and generous offer of salvation? It is pride, the deadliest of all the deadly sins. Bernard Shaw, an example of a modern-day thinker, said: "Forgiveness is a beggar's refuge. We must pay our debts." *But we cannot pay our debts.* As our spiritual fathers saw so clearly, the only language we can use in the presence of a God who demands so much and whose demands we are unable to meet is:

*Just as I am without one plea
But that Thy blood was shed for me,
And that Thou bidd'st me come to Thee,
O Lamb of God, I come, I come.*

In response to our coming, the free unmerited favor of God flows down to us, cancels our debt, imputes and imparts Christ's righteousness to us. How can Christ's righteousness be imputed and imparted to us? It's *His* righteousness, not ours. A simple illustration may help to illuminate this point. A dull little boy came home from school one day and said to his mother: "*We've* won a holiday." The truth was another boy had come top of the region in the examinations and the head teacher decided to give the whole school a holiday. Yet the dull little lad said: "We've won a holiday."

Grace is like that. God permits the righteousness of Jesus to cover us and then, as we open ourselves to it – to enter us. *He* did it, but *we* benefit from it. Isn't grace *really* amazing?

FURTHER STUDY

Phil. 4:1–19;
1 Tim. 1:14;
Titus 3:6

1. What has God promised?
2. What did Paul testify to Timothy?

⇢ *Prayer* ⇠

O Father, as I contemplate still further the "riches" of Your grace, once again I have to confess it's truly amazing. No wonder men and women use that term to describe Your grace. No other adjective will do! Amen.

The God of all grace

"But by the grace of God I am what I am ..." (v.10)

For reading & meditation – 1 Corinthians 15:1–11

*I*s it any wonder that throughout the history of the Christian Church men and women have found the thought of grace so overwhelmingly wonderful they seemed unable to get over it? Grace was the constant theme of their prayers, their preaching, their writing – and their hymns. Take this for example:

> *Great God of wonders, all Thy ways*
> *Display the attributes divine;*
> *But countless acts of pardoning grace*
> *Beyond Thine other wonders shine;*
> *Who is a pardoning God like Thee?*
> *Or who has grace so rich and free?*

Many have fought to uphold the truth of God's grace, accepting ridicule and loss of privilege as the price of their stand. Paul waged war against the legalists in the Galatian churches over the matter of "grace," and the battle to uphold this great truth has gone on ever since. Augustine fought it in the fourth and fifth centuries, and so did the Reformers in the sixteenth century.

I sense that the Church once again is in danger of losing out to legalism as more and more Christians get caught up with *doing* rather than *being*. Talk to people about what they are doing and they are with you at once; talk to them about being (who they really are) and their attitude is one of deferential blankness. The Church of Jesus Christ is in a sad state when it can't say with conviction and meaning, as did the apostle Paul: "By the grace of God I am what I am."

FURTHER STUDY

2 Cor. 1:1–12; 6:1;
Gal. 2:21

1. Where was Paul's boast rooted?

2. What was Paul's warning to the Corinthians?

⊹⊹ *Prayer* ⊹⊹

"God of all grace, give me grace to feel my need of grace. And give me grace to ask for grace. Then give me grace to receive grace. And when grace is given to me, give me grace to use that grace." In Jesus' Name I pray. Amen.

God knows all

"... I know what is going through your mind." (v.5)
For reading & meditation – Ezekiel 11:1–15

The final aspect of God's nature that we examine is His knowledge and wisdom. I link these two characteristics together because really it is almost impossible to consider one without considering the other. This is true of all God's attributes, but perhaps more so of the two we are now about to consider.

The difference between knowledge and wisdom has been described like this: "Knowledge is what we know; wisdom is the right application of what we know." God, of course, knows everything; everything possible; everything actual. He is perfectly acquainted with every detail in the life of every being in heaven, in earth, and in hell. Daniel said of Him: "He knows what lies in darkness, and light dwells with him" (Dan. 2:22). Nothing escapes His notice, nothing can be hidden from Him, and nothing can be forgotten by Him. I know that many Christians when referring to their conversion say that God has forgotten their sins, but strictly speaking that is not so. God never forgets anything. What He promises to do with our sins is "to remember [them] no more" (Jer. 31:34). There is a great difference between forgetting something and deciding not to remember it.

Realising, as we do, that God knows everything ought to strengthen our faith and cause us to bow in adoration before Him. The hymnist put it effectively when he wrote:

> *The knowledge of this life is small,*
> *The eye of faith is dim,*
> *But 'tis enough that God knows all*
> *And I shall be with Him.*

FURTHER STUDY

Job 31:1–4; 34:21–25;
Psa. 147:5

1. What was Job's question?

2. What was Elihu's response?

❖ *Prayer* ❖

O Father, how consoling it is to know that You know everything. Nothing ever escapes Your attention. This means I can relax, for what I don't know You know. And because You know it, then what I don't know can't hurt me. Amen.

Reflect on perfection

*"They will speak of the glorious splendor of your majesty,
and I will meditate on your wonderful works." (v.5)*

For reading & meditation – Psalm 145:1–20

We ended yesterday by saying that the fact God knows everything ought to strengthen our faith and cause us to bow in adoration before Him. Yet how little do we reflect on this divine perfection. Those who are inclined to rebel against God hate this aspect of His Being and would do away with it if they could. They wish there might be no Witness to their sin, no Searcher of their hearts, no Judge of their deeds. How solemn are the words of the psalmist recorded in Psalm 90:8: "You have set our iniquities before you, our secret sins in the light of your presence."

To the believer, however, the truth of God's omniscience (all knowledge) ought to be one of tremendous comfort and security. In times of perplexity we ought to say like Job: "He knows the way that I take; when he has tested me, I shall come forth as gold" (Job 23:10). Whatever might be going on in our lives that is profoundly mysterious to us and quite incomprehensible to those who are around us, we must never lose sight of the fact that "He knows the way that [we] take." Right down the running ages God's people have consoled themselves time and time again with the fact that God knows everything about them. The psalmist, when seeking to stir his soul to confidence and hope, reminded himself in the midst of his weakness and weariness: "He knows how we are formed, he remembers that we are dust" (Psa. 103:14). And Simon Peter, when his failure brought him almost to the point of despair and the searching question came "Do you love me?" said: "Lord, you *know* all things; you *know* that I love you" (John 21:17).

FURTHER STUDY

Isa. 55:1–9;
Heb. 4:12–13;
1 John 3:20

1. What statement did God make?
2. What did the writer to the Hebrews confirm?

⊷ *Prayer* ⊷

Father, help me reflect on this fact that You know everything, for I see that the more I understand it the more secure I will feel in my soul. Teach me still more, dear Lord. In Jesus' Name. Amen.

The God who sees

"... I have now seen the One who sees me." (v.13)
For reading & meditation – Genesis 16:1–16

hat matters most – that I know God or that God knows me? I think in a sense the latter. For my knowledge of Him depends on His sustained initiative in knowing me. Just as the knowledge of His love for me causes the scales to fall from my eyes and turns the machinery of my soul in His direction, so my knowledge of how intimately He knows me does something similar. I am graven on the palms of His hands. I am never out of His thoughts. He knows me as a friend and there is not a single moment when His eye is not upon me.

It was this that Hagar came to see when she was feeling utterly bereft and forgotten – that God saw her and knew everything there was to know about her. "I have now seen the One who sees me," she said. There is unspeakable comfort in knowing that God knows all about us.

Dietrich Bonhoeffer was a German pastor who was executed by the Nazis. During the days prior to his death the thing that brought him great solace was not so much that he knew God, but that God knew him. The poem he wrote in his prison cell entitled "Who am I?" ends with the words *"who* am I? O Lord Thou knowest I am *thine."* Knowing how much he was known by God brought him great comfort and consolation. He knew that whatever happened to him, it would not happen without God's knowledge.

FURTHER STUDY

Psa. 119:161–168;
Nah. 1:7;
1 Cor. 8:3;
2 Tim. 2:19

1. What was the psalmist able to acknowledge?

2. What sort of person is known by God?

⋯⋯ Prayer ⋯⋯

Gracious and loving Lord, thank You for reminding me that my knowledge of You depends on Your knowledge of me. Your knowledge of me stirs my soul toward my knowing You. You initiate – I respond. Keep initiating, dear Lord. In Jesus' Name. Amen.

Fullness – only in God

*"... to the only wise God be glory forever through
Jesus Christ!" (v.27)*

For reading & meditation – Romans 16:17–27

The subject of God's knowledge must be linked to His wisdom, and it is this aspect of the divine nature that we consider now. What does the Bible mean when it describes God as wise? It means the ability to use knowledge to the best possible ends. This ability is found in its fullness only in God. God is never other than wise in everything He does. Knowledge without wisdom would be pathetic; a broken reed. Wisdom without knowledge would be inoperative and quite frightening. God's boundless knowledge and wisdom are perfect in every way, and it is this that makes Him utterly worthy of our trust.

One of the great difficulties we have in the Christian life is trusting the divine wisdom. We can recognize wisdom only when we see the end to which it is moving. God often calls us to trust Him when we can't see the end that He is pursuing, and then in such times we have to ask ourselves: How much do I trust Him?

Before I began speaking to a Christian youth group once, I asked if someone could offer a definition of God's wisdom. One young man said: "God's wisdom is the ability to get us through scrapes and difficulties without getting hurt." I gave the young man full marks for attempting a definition, but I had to show him that was not what divine wisdom is all about. God's wisdom is not and never was pledged to getting us through life without being hurt. The goal behind divine wisdom is not to make us happy but to make us holy. And sometimes pursuing that goal may involve us in considerable pain.

FURTHER STUDY

Psa. 104:1–24;
Prov. 3:19;
Rom. 11:33

1. Where is God's wisdom evidenced?

2. What was Paul's conclusion?

⊷ *Prayer* ⊷

Father, here I am again – at the road less travelled. Help me tread the road ahead knowing whatever pain You allow me to feel is for my good. I do not welcome it, but I do not run from it either, as long as You stay with me. Amen.

DAY 177

God's one great goal

"For those God foreknew he also predestined to be conformed to the likeness of his Son ..." (v.29)

For reading & meditation – Romans 8:28–39

What is God's great goal in the universe to which His energies are devoted? We have it in our text for today. The Living Bible puts this best and I have no hesitation in saying that although it is not regarded as a true translation (it is rather a paraphrase), its rendering of Romans 8:29 is one of the most exciting things I have ever read. This is what it says: "For from the very beginning God decided that those who came to him ... should *become* like his Son." God's great energy and wisdom, working on behalf of all Christians, is directed to making us like His Son Jesus Christ. Of course this purpose will only be fully realized in the world to come, but while we are here He is pursuing that selfsame purpose nevertheless.

It is only when we comprehend this that we will be able to understand the purpose that lies behind all our trials and difficulties. Romans 8:28 – "And we know that all that happens to us is working for our good" (TLB) – must be read in connection with Romans 8:29. Because God is committed to making us like His Son, His wisdom goes to work on every trial that comes our way in order to bring from it something that will enrich our character and make us more like Jesus Christ. Infinite power is ruled by infinite wisdom. He could deliver us and make our lives comfortable but in a fallen world that is not the *best* purpose. Understanding this is crucial if we are to live our lives the way God desires.

FURTHER STUDY

1 Cor. 1:1–31;
Col. 2:3

1. How does Paul describe the foolishness of God?

2. What is hidden in Christ?

⊷ *Prayer* ⊷

Father, forgive me that so often my goals are diametrically opposed to Yours. Help me bring my goals in line with Your goals. I shall need Your help to adjust. Whatever happens, keep me ever moving toward becoming more and more like Jesus. Amen.

"Some extra practice"

*"Consider it pure joy, my brothers, whenever you face
trials of many kinds ..." (v.2)*

For reading & meditation – James 1:1–18

The Bible is replete with instances of God's wisdom moving men and women through the most difficult times to the most wonderful ends. Take Abraham for example. Although he is known in Scripture as the "the friend of God," he was capable of some shabby behavior. On one occasion he actually compromised his wife's chastity (Gen. 12:10–20), and later, submitting to her pressure, fathered a child by Hagar, their maid (Gen. 16:1–16). Then, seeking to avoid Sarah's hysterical recriminations, he allowed her to drive Hagar away from their household (Gen. 21:8–21). Clearly, Abraham was not a man of strong principle and there were great flaws in his character. But God in wisdom dealt with this man and brought him through some great trials until he was changed from a man of the world to a true man of God.

The same wisdom which ordered the path Abraham trod orders our lives. We should never be taken aback when unexpected and upsetting things happen to us. We should recognize that no matter how hard the trial, God's power will be there to get us through, and God's wisdom will ensure that the trial will be worth more than it costs. I like the almost tongue-in-cheek way Jim Packer describes what may be God's design when He permits us to go through trials: "Perhaps he means to strengthen us in patience, good humor, compassion, humility, or meekness by giving us some extra practice in exercising these graces under specially difficult situations." *"Some extra practice."* Some of us, myself included, sorely need it.

FURTHER STUDY

Isa. 48:1–10;
Psa. 66:10;
Mal. 3:3;
1 Pet. 1:7

1. What process is God's
testing likened to?

2. What is the end
result?

⤙ *Prayer* ⤚

Father, help me grasp this truth once and for all, that Your wisdom ensures the trials I go through are worth far more than they cost. You are more committed to making me like Jesus than I am myself. It hurts sometimes, but deep down I am grateful. Amen.

Our only hope

*"... I am the Lord, who exercizes kindness, justice
and righteousness on earth ..." (v.24)*

For reading & meditation – Jeremiah 9:17–24

Let's review what we have said about God's character. We began by recognizing that in today's Church we seem more interested in knowing about ourselves than in knowing God. The result of being more man-centered than God-centered is increased anxiety, depression, and a hundred other ills. Quietly we have worked through the Scriptures and have seen that the God who is "there" for us to know is the God who has revealed Himself in many different ways: as powerful, personal, plural, having holy love, a God of wrath, trustworthy, gracious, all-knowing and all-wise.

It's interesting isn't it, as our passage for today shows, that when the Lord talks about Himself in the Scriptures it is usually in terms of His attributes or character traits: kindness, justice, righteousness, and so on. And there is a clear and definite purpose in this: the more we know of God the more established our lives will be here on the earth. I myself am convinced that there is nothing more important than knowing God through contemplation of Him. And it must be understood that the knowledge I am talking about is not mere intellectual knowledge. The knowledge of God that comes through contemplation of Him is the ability to see life from His perspective, through His eyes. It means to look out at life's circumstances through the lens of faith, bearing in mind God's plan, to accept that whatever is happening is allowed by God and that everything comes under His personal surveillance. That kind of God-understanding and God-awareness is our only hope for coping with twentieth-century problems.

FURTHER STUDY

**Phil. 3:1–11;
Col. 1:9–10**

1. What was Paul's desire?
2. What did Paul pray for the Colossians?

❧ *Prayer* ❧

Father, I am convinced. I see that if I am to operate in a context of confidence I can only do so as I look out at life through Your eyes. Help me to do more than glance at You occasionally. Help me to gaze on You continually. Amen.

The truth in a nutshell

"... the people who know their God will firmly resist him." (v.32)
For reading & meditation – Daniel 11:14–35

What are the benefits of keeping our gaze continually focused on God? I can think of at least three. First, the more we study Him the more we will want to become like Him. The most natural thing in the world when there is a good relationship between parents and their children is for that child to want to become like them. That is the way it is also with God our Father. The more we discover of His love, His holiness, His purity, His trustworthiness, His strength, His patience, the more we want to emulate Him.

Second, the more we study God the better we will know ourselves. When Isaiah stepped into the Temple and had a vision of God, he also saw the truth about himself. Things that were hidden deep within him came to light in the presence of the Eternal.

Third, the more we study Him the clearer will be our perspective on the world. When you see that God is in charge then you won't panic every time you open the newspaper. You can only know God, of course, through Christ, and because You have Him, instead of saying, "Look what the world has come to," you will be able to say: "Look what has come to the world."

The people who know their God will firmly resist the Adversary, says Daniel. The Amplified Bible puts it well: "... the people who know their God shall prove themselves strong and shall stand firm and do exploits." I can do no more than to say – there you have it in a nutshell. The more you know God the stronger you will be.

FURTHER STUDY

2 Tim. 1:1–12;
John 17:3;
Job 19:25

1. What did Jesus pray?

2. What was the key to Job's facing his difficult circumstances?

⭢ *Prayer* ⭠

My Father and my God, now I set my course for the wide seas. With Your truth as my compass, and Your Word as my chart, I set sail on this great adventure – to know You better. I can count on You but can I count on me? With Christ's help I can. In Jesus' Name. Amen.

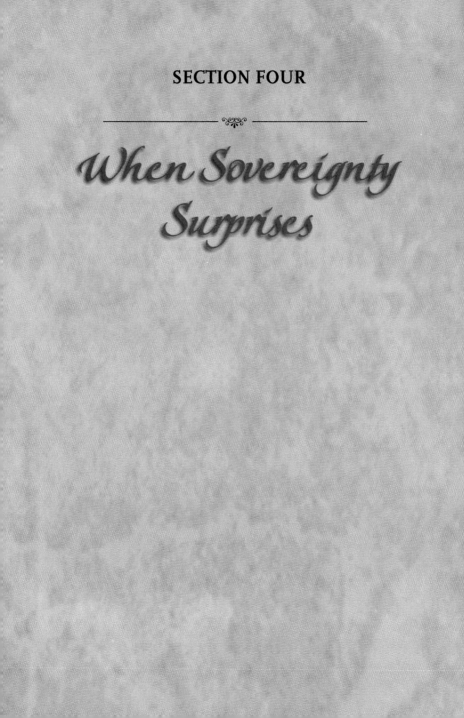

SECTION FOUR

*When Sovereignty
Surprises*

When Sovereignty Surprises

———— ❦ ————

*P*eople sometimes ask Thomas Kinkade why, as a Christian, he doesn't paint what they think of as "religious subjects." He explains that it's because he sees God in every moment of life, everywhere he looks. A dewdrop on a rosebud, or the golden sunset on the rim of a cloud has religious significance to him because each is one of God's little miracles. The Creator reveals Himself through His perfect handiwork all around us.

The studies in this section of *Every Day Light* are similar examples of His presence in that they remind us of how God sometimes reveals Himself in indirect and surprising ways. These lessons concentrate on books about two great women of the Bible, Ruth and Esther. Both narratives are filled with unexpected twists and turns as the women face seemingly unsolvable problems.

In each case, God works almost imperceptibly to bring about dramatic changes over time. The tragic outcome we expect is reversed when ordinary people accomplish extraordinary things as a result of God's indirect involvement.

Esther is the only book in the Bible that never mentions God. But He is clearly there just the same in the story of this great Persian queen who saves the Jewish people from destruction. The famous reversal of fortune between Haman and Mordecai is a compelling example of a divine hand working from behind the scene.

Esther's faith is rewarded, as is Ruth's. Along with her sister and mother, Ruth faces a bleak future as a widow in a society where all wealth and property pass through the male line. Yet all three are soon to be redeemed and, through Ruth, become ancestors of David, the greatest king in the history of Israel.

Even when He seems absent from the scene, God ultimately brings victory for the faithful.

L.G.G.

I belong

"Boaz the father of Obed, whose mother was Ruth ..." (v.5)

For reading & meditation – Matthew 1:1–17

*O*ur theme now centers on the only two books in the Bible which are named after women – Esther and Ruth. Although the two books are quite different in style and scope, there are several intriguing similarities. First, both books depict a woman who was brought by God into an unusual marriage. Second, both books are set against a background of great national peril. Third, both books teach us valuable lessons about the providential dealings of a great and loving God.

We focus first on the story of Ruth. The first thing we must notice about Ruth is that her name is included in Matthew's genealogy of our Lord Jesus Christ. It was the custom in Israel when writing out a genealogy to list only the names of men, but occasionally, if there was a special reason to do so, the names of women were included. Good and godly though Ruth was, however, the real reason why her name is mentioned here is because she was among those who were the direct antecedents of the Lord Jesus Christ. She, as well as the others, are given prominence not because of what they had achieved but because of who they were related to – Jesus.

It is a parable. Our real greatness in this world arises not so much from what we do but from whether or not we are directly related to Christ. When we are linked by faith to Him we are given a status that lifts us above the greatest of earth's categories. This is where real significance lies – in being related to Him. Never forget – you are who you are because He is who He is.

FURTHER STUDY

Gal. 4:1–7;
Rom. 8:17;
Mark 3:31, 34

1. What status has God given us?

2. How did Jesus describe His relationship to us?

⇢ *Prayer* ⇠

O Father, how can I ever thank You enough for bringing me into a relationship with Yourself and with Your Son? I belong – belong to You and thus to everyone else who belongs to You. I am so deeply, deeply grateful. Amen.

DAY

182

Spiritual dryness

*"In those days Israel had no king; everyone
did as he saw fit." (v.6)*

For reading & meditation – Judges 17:1–13

uth arrived on the scene in the period when the judges
ruled in Israel. The children of Israel had occupied the
land for some time. But the peace and prosperity that had
been theirs disappeared after Joshua's death, when the people
returned to their evil and disobedient ways. The condition of
Israel at the time Ruth appears was, as our text for today points
out, that "everyone did as he saw fit."

As a direct consequence of this rebellion there was famine in
the land – physical and spiritual. When men and women turn
from God and persist in doing what is right in their own eyes,
barrenness and dryness follows – as surely as night follows day.

Am I talking to someone right now whose spiritual life is
empty and dry? You read the Bible dutifully every day but its
words do not speak to you as once they did. There is always a
reason for spiritual dryness. It doesn't just happen. A sense of
spiritual dryness can arise from a poor physical condition. More
usually, though, it comes about because something has gone
wrong spiritually. If you are feeling dry and barren in your spirit
at this moment, and you are convinced it does not stem from a
physical condition, then ask yourself: Is there some disobedience
in my life that needs to be recognized and repented of? The saying
"He who will not heed the helm must heed the rocks" is certainly
true. Unless we live in obedience to Christ and His commands,
then we will have to settle for a life that is less than the best.

FURTHER STUDY

Isa. ch. 35;
Matt. 12:20

1. What did Jesus say
concerning those who
are burned out or
broken?

2. What highway
are we called to
walk upon?

→→ *Prayer* ←←

---

*O God, I know that Your way always leads to fruitfulness, sparkle and joy. In
the hour of spiritual dryness help me to track down its cause and then turn to
the cure – real and radical repentance. In Jesus' Name I pray. Amen.*

The danger of expediency

*"A man ... together with his wife and two sons,
went to live ... in the country of Moab." (v.1)*

For reading & meditation – Ruth 1:1–2

As the famine of which we spoke yesterday continues to ravage Israel, Elimelech and his little family make the decision to emigrate to the land of Moab. Was this a right decision – or a wrong one? Bible students have debated this question for centuries.

The Moabites were the result of the incestuous union between Lot and his daughters (Gen. 19:29–38). They appeared to be a bad bunch who always opposed Israel. On one occasion they refused the Israelites bread and water, and hired Balaam to curse them. Because of this, God forbade the Moabites to come into the presence of the Lord, and told the Israelites not to seek their peace or their prosperity (Deut. 23:3–7).

Elimelech's decision to move his family into Moab may have appeared to be a good choice economically, but I believe it was a bad choice spiritually. He went directly against God's commands. Of course it can be argued that when one considers the positive things that came out of the move – the book of Ruth for example – then what they did was right. But when we see good coming out of something, we must never assume that God willed it that way; rather, He works through the bad to make all things contribute to His glory. Christians should never try to foresee the results of an action and thus justify going against God's commands. Instead, it should be the constant practice of every Christian to decide everything on the basis of God's will as displayed in His Word. We live dangerously when we allow expediency, and not the clear guidelines of Scripture, to determine our actions and our directions.

FURTHER STUDY

Psa.119:1–12; 97–112;
1 Pet. 1:25

1. What had the psalmist done in order not to sin?

2. What had the psalmist chosen?

Prayer

O Father, burn into my consciousness the things I have read today so that I will never be directed by expediency but by the clear directions that come out of Your Word. In Jesus' Name I ask it. Amen.

Putting God first

"Now Elimelech, Naomi's husband, died, and she was left with her two sons." (v.3)

For reading & meditation – Ruth 1:3–5

Although Elimelech's decision to care and provide for his family must be applauded, there can be little doubt that in moving to the land of Moab he went against the will of God. Everything seemed to go well at first, and no doubt the improved economic conditions were to their liking. One day, however, tragedy strikes. Elimelech is taken ill and dies. Naomi, his wife, now faces the devastation of bereavement. Later, her two sons – both of whom had taken Moabite wives – also die, and she has to bear the pain of this further tragedy. These circumstances reinforce the point we made yesterday about the folly of making decisions based on expediency rather than on the will of God. How prone we are to allow materialistic or economic values to influence our judgment.

A man and his family emigrated, lured by the appeal of financial security. He wrote: "Would to God I had thought of the spiritual implications before I made the move. My life and family are in ruins." This is why it is always wise to pray over a move to another town, city or country, as there may be unseen dangers that are revealed only through prayer.

A change of circumstances will not necessarily solve our problems. We think if we had a new home, a new church, a new husband or wife, a new minister, or a new job, that all our difficulties would be over. As Christians, every major decision we make ought to be set against God's perfect will. We owe it to God to bring Him into our decision making. Otherwise we may find we have gained economically but lost out spiritually.

FURTHER STUDY

Josh. 24:1–15;
Micah 4:5;
Luke 10:42

1. What conclusion did Joshua come to?

2. What did Jesus say of Mary?

Prayer

My Father and my God, help me never to allow economic or personal considerations to influence my judgment when making life's major decisions. Grant that I might subject all my decisions and movements to Your perfect will. In Jesus' Name. Amen.

Forgive yourself!

*"Naomi and her daughters-in-law prepared
to return home ..." (v.6)*

For reading & meditation – Ruth 1:6–13

After Naomi has recovered from the shock of losing her husband and two sons in the land of Moab, she hears that Israel is once again a flourishing land and she makes up her mind to return to her people. When she announces her intentions to her daughters-in-law, Ruth and Orpah, they decide to accompany her on the journey home. As the three make their way out of Moab, Naomi feels it necessary to point out to the young women that their chances of finding someone to marry in Canaan would be very remote. What mother in Israel would allow her son to marry a woman from Moab? Naomi makes it clear that if she had other sons who were eligible for marriage, she would gladly give them to her two bereaved daughters-in-law, but as this is not so she encourages them to return to their own homes.

At this point Naomi seems saddened and overwhelmed by all that has happened and utters these solemn words: "It is more bitter for me than for you, because the Lord's hand has gone out against me" (v.13). We must be careful not to read too much into this statement, but I feel that there were some feelings of self-recrimination reverberating beneath that remark. Naomi, being an Israelite, would have known how to approach God for forgiveness. However, it would appear that she has not yet forgiven herself. Self-pity and self-contempt are always signals that say one has not really received the divine forgiveness. Whenever you are in need of forgiveness, open your soul to receive it, and then make sure you do not short-circuit the spiritual system by failing to forgive yourself.

FURTHER STUDY

Rom. 8:1–4;
1 John 3:19–20;
Matt. 26:75;
Gal. 5:1

1. What are we to stand firm in?

2. How did Peter handle his remorse?

⇥ *Prayer* ⇤

Heavenly Father, I see how easy it is to allow sorrow for my sin to become self-reproach or self-pity. Help me, whenever I am in need of forgiveness, to receive it from You, and then to forgive myself. In Jesus' Name I pray. Amen.

DAY

186

The leap of faith

"Where you go I will go, and where you stay I will stay." (v.16)

For reading & meditation – Ruth 1:14–18

fter Naomi's advice to her daughters-in-law that they should stay in Moab, Orpah, albeit reluctantly, prepares to return home. So deep however is Ruth's love for her mother-in-law that she begs to be allowed to accompany her to Israel, in one of the most moving passages in the Old Testament.

Ruth is well aware that great problems will face her when she arrives in Israel – national, cultural and religious. But her determination to remain at the side of her mother-in-law is so great that she pours out her feelings in these words: "Where you go I will go, and where you stay I will stay." Such is her love for Naomi that the possibility that they might have no permanent home makes no difference whatsoever. "Your people will be my people." Imagine giving up your friends and family to settle in a land where you know you could well be ostracized. "And your God my God." Ruth had evidently seen and heard enough from Naomi to realize that the God of the Israelites was Someone worth knowing.

FURTHER STUDY

John 6:25–70;
Matt. 16:13–20

1, What did Peter declare about Jesus?

2. What was his response to Jesus?

What a magnificent picture this is of a true conversion. Ruth and Orpah stand at the crossroads. Orpah draws back to end her days in the darkness of heathen idolatry, while Ruth moves on to a new land and a new future, and to have her name inscribed forever on the sacred record. How sad that so many can appear to be deeply religious, travel for a time with God's people, yet fail to make that "leap of faith" that entrusts all one has and all one is to the Savior. If you have not done so, make the leap of faith today.

✦ *Prayer* ✦

Gracious and loving Father, help me understand that keeping company with Your people is not enough for salvation. I must make that determined leap of faith. I do so now. Receive me and make me Yours. In Jesus' Name. Amen.

The marks of disobedience

"The Lord has afflicted me; the Almighty has brought misfortune upon me." (v.21)

For reading & meditation – Ruth 1:19-22

*A*fter the long journey from Moab, Naomi, in company with her daughter-in-law, Ruth, finally reaches Bethlehem. There she is welcomed by the whole community, who seemingly turn out in force to greet her. One can deduce from the question "Can this be Naomi?" (v.19) something of the change that must have taken place in her appearance. Undoubtedly, the circumstances through which she had passed, and the sojourn in Moab, had left deep marks upon her. Naomi's response is swift, and still tinged with self-recrimination: "Don't call me Naomi [sweet or pleasant] ... Call me Mara [unpleasant], because the Almighty has made my life very bitter." Although there might have been some feelings of self-recrimination in Naomi's heart, the fact must not be overlooked that she was also a living testimony of what happens to those who choose some way other than God's way. "Those who take God's way," says Dr. E. Stanley Jones, "get results. Those who don't get consequences."

I have met many who stepped out of the will of God, and although they returned to Him and were forgiven, they still carry in their bodies and personalities the consequences of their actions. I heard of a Christian who, finding he had homosexual tendencies, decided to engage in one homosexual encounter – just to see what it would be like. He contracted AIDS, and unless the Lord heals him or a cure is found, he will probably die. We ought to remember that if we move away from the will of God, the sin in which we engage can be forgiven, but the marks of sin may remain in us and upon us for a lifetime.

FURTHER STUDY

Ex. 15:20-27;
Psa. 23

1. What happened at Marah?

2. Where did God lead Israel?

Prayer

Father, I see that in this world I can either get results – or consequences. Help me not to go against the grain of the universe, for life is designed to move in one way – Your way. Teach me to walk in Your statutes. Amen.

Maximizing time

"Naomi had a relative on her husband's side ... a man of standing, whose name was Boaz." (v.1)

For reading & meditation – Ruth 2:1

his one verse is like a window through which light floods to illuminate Naomi's family background. It tells us that her deceased husband, Elimelech, came from a wealthy family, and that now most of that wealth was in the hands of a young relative of Elimelech's – Boaz.

We know from the preceding verse (Ruth 1:22) that Naomi and Ruth have arrived in Bethlehem just as the harvest is about to begin. Ruth sets about the task of finding something to do. People of character always have a mind to work. Continued laziness, unless physiologically based, is evidence that a person's character is flawed. He or she is non-contributive and thus will not discover, as one of the laws of life says, that "It is more blessed to give than to receive." If you want some interesting hours in the Bible, look up the passages where God appears to people and calls them to special service. You will find that in most cases, if not in every case, when He came to them they were already busily engaged in some task. Moses was tending the sheep. Amos received his call while walking behind a plow. Peter, James, John and Andrew were called to Christ's service when mending their nets. Some idly sit around waiting for God to call them to special service and wonder why they never hear His voice. God is looking to see how we are handling the ordinary tasks of life before He entrusts us with the special things. Put your whole energy into every task that comes your way and perhaps God will give you the opportunity to do bigger and greater things.

FURTHER STUDY

Matt. 25:14–23;
Luke 16:10;
1 Cor. 4:1–2

1. Why did the master put the servant in charge of many things?

2. What are we to be faithful in?

⊷♦ *Prayer* ♦⊷

My Father and my God, help me see that the little tasks, when done well, qualify me for the bigger tasks that may be up ahead. May I turn to today's duties with enthusiasm and dedication. For today may be the day when I am called to bigger things. Amen.

Unconscious guidance

"So she went out and began to glean in the fields behind the harvesters." (v.3)

For reading & meditation – Ruth 2:2–3

Ruth has no difficulty in finding a task to gainfully occupy her for, as we read in Ruth 1:22, they arrived in Bethlehem "as the barley harvest was beginning."

At harvest time there was always work to be found in the fields, even if it was only gathering up after the reapers. When the workers went through the fields reaping the harvest, often, because of the speed at which they worked, they would leave behind small unreaped sections. These unreaped areas were then covered by "gleaners," who would walk behind and reap the grain that was still standing. Jewish law stated that the gleanings must be left for the poor, and the grain collected by the gleaners became theirs (Lev. 19:9–10; Deut. 24:19). During the harvest, all the fields were open to be gleaned. No employment agency. No special selection system. No union cards. Those who had the need and desire to glean simply went and worked wherever the inclination took them.

As Ruth takes up the role of gleaner, she happens to find herself reaping in one of the fields which belonged to Boaz. The term used in the second half of our text for today, "as it turned out," is filled with deep spiritual meaning. Divine guidance was at work here. Ruth might not have realized it or sensed it, for most divine guidance takes place when we are not conscious of it.

FURTHER STUDY

Luke 12:4–12;
Psa. 115:12;
Matt. 6:25–34;
Isa. 46:4

1. Why are we not to worry about life?

2. What is God's promise through Isaiah?

⊱ *Prayer* ⊰

Father, forgive me for the times I have thought things have happened to me because of luck, when really it has been the Lord. How glad I am that I am being guided not by the stars but by the Savior. I am truly thankful. Amen.

Nothing too trivial

"As it turned out, she found herself working in a field belonging to Boaz ..." (v.3)

For reading & meditation – Ruth 2:3

We spend another day considering how Ruth finds herself gleaning a field which belonged to Boaz, not by chance but by divine guidance. Eliezer, Abraham's servant, you remember, experienced similar leading when he went to search for a bride for Isaac: "I being in the way, the Lord led me" (Gen. 24:27, KJV).

The fact that God should condescend to guide us in this life is wonderful, but nothing can be more wonderful than guidance of which we are not conscious. How reassuring it is to know that even when we are not seeking it, God is guiding us still. I am sure that almost every one of you can look back and recollect a time when, because of a "chance" occurrence, your life took a completely different turn. The world explains these things as coincidences, and sometimes they are no more than that, but there are special times when seeming coincidences are really God-instances. The Almighty is at work, bringing His wondrous purposes to pass.

This is because, as the theologians tell us, God not only has a general providence – one in which all His creation benefits – but a special providence which involves only those who have a personal relationship with God through His Son Jesus Christ (Rom. 8:28). After a lifetime of knowing God's special providence, the great Samuel Chadwick, one-time principal of Cliff College in Derbyshire, England, said: "The divine attention to detail is amazing. Nothing is too trivial for Omnipotence." Though the universe revolves at His word, He means it when He says to you and me: "I will guide thee with mine eye" (Psa. 32:8, KJV).

FURTHER STUDY

Psa. 48; 73:24;
Isa. 30:21; 42:16

1. What was the psalmist's conviction?

2. What has God promised for the rough, dark and unfamiliar places?

⊷ Prayer ⊶

O Father, how humbling yet how encouraging it is to know that You guide me even when I am not conscious of it. Forgive me that I do not thank You enough for this. But I do so now. Thank You dear Father. Thank You. Amen.